Very Simple
ARABIA

Very Simple
ARABIA

Written and illustrated

by

James Peters

VERY SIMPLE ARABIA

Published by
Stacey International
128 Kensington Church Street
London W8 4BH
Tel: +44 (0)20 7221 7166
Fax: +44 (0)20 7792 9288
E-mail: marketing@stacey-international.co.uk
www.stacey-international.co.uk

Reprinted 2012

3 5 7 9 8 6 4

ISBN: 978-1-905299-51-5

Printed in Singapore

British Library Catalogue in Publication Data:
A catalogue record for this book is available from the British Library.

Very Simple Arabia is a simple but complete guide to the region of the Gulf States, Saudi Arabia, Oman and Yemen.

Foreigners visiting this area for the first time will find themselves in a world which in many respects is profoundly unfamiliar. The most sympathetic person will find the scene confusing. The language is complicated, the social etiquette, by which the Arabs set so much store, takes time to pick up and the Muslim religion is everywhere in evidence. Finally, the whole is shrouded in that indefinable element, the mystique of the orient.

Very Simple Arabia sets out to present the subject in an easily understandable form. It outlines the geography, history, language, etiquette, religion, modern society, government and business of the region – information essential to a grasp of the place, its peoples and its culture.

For those wishing to know more about the Arabic language and the script the reader's attention is invited to the two sister volumes of this book – *Very Simple Arabic* and *Very Simple Arabic Script*.

JAMES PETERS

Acknowledgements

The publishers and I express our thanks to those who have kindly given advice in the making of this book: in particular Hussein Dabbagh; Dr S. Darsh, former Imam of the London Mosque; Patrick de Courcy-Ireland CVO; Paul Mahmood; Richard Palmer; Frederick Sullivan; Lawrie Walker LVO, OBE; and Yaqub Yousuf.

J.P.

Contents

A Note on Pronunciation

Arabic words – written in italics – are intended to be pronounced exactly as the English spelling suggests, except that:

aa	is pronounced as		'a' in 'father'
ow	"	"	'ow' in 'how'
u	"	"	'u' in 'put'
dh	"	"	'th' in 'the'
kh	"	"	'ch' in 'loch'
gh	"	"	'r' in French 'rue'
ei	"	"	'eye'
q	"	"	a guttural 'k'
'	"	"	a glottal stop

There are no capital letters in Arabic. Where necessary, the stress syllable is shown in bold type and doubled consonants should be given extra stress. Finally, the definite article '*al*' is linked to its noun or adjective by a hyphen.

Although any written guide to pronunciation will have its limitations and most beginners are naturally shy about speaking words which are unfamiliar, do not be put off. Have a go! Arabs are used to hearing a variety of accents, even from within the Arab world and will generally be delighted that you have made the effort. Do not take correction as criticism – it will improve your fluency and establish a rapport.

1

Arabia

Arabia is the historical name for that part of the Arab world which today comprises . . .

. . . Saudi Arabia, the Gulf states, Oman and Yemen*. It is also called The Arabian Peninsula – in Arabic *al-jaz**ee**ra al-ara**bia***.

* Information on individual countries is given in the Country Annexes on page 89.

As most people might imagine, the major features of the Arabian terrain are the great sand deserts – the Nefud and the vast Rub Al-Khali (The Empty Quarter). In addition, gravel-covered desert plains extend over the central region, and along the Gulf coast in the east there is low-lying desert with ***sub**kha* or salt flats.

However, Western Arabia features the mountain ranges of the Hijaz and Asir which run the length of the Red Sea coast and rise into the mountains of Yemen. In the northeast, in Oman, are the Hajar mountains which include the famous Jebel Akhdar (Green Mountain).

There are also some significant areas of cultivation, particularly in Asir, the Yemen Highlands and Oman as well as numerous oases.

The huge Al-Hasa oasis in Saudi Arabia is the largest in the world.

Nevertheless, water is scarce – increasingly so. Although modern cities use desalinated water, which also supports parks and gardens using efficient irrigation techniques, ground water is extensively tapped for cultivation and domestic use and water table levels are falling.

A high priority is given to conservation and environmental projects with the establishment of nature reserves and breeding programmes for endangered species such as the Arabian Oryx.

However, the first time visitor to Arabia is likely to be most impressed by its modern cities and developed infrastructure – all of which have been accomplished in the last forty years.

Among numerous architectural achievements are the spectacular Burj Al-Arab (Arab Tower) in Dubai...

And the 26 kilometre long King Fahd Causeway linking the Kingdoms of Saudi Arabia and Bahrain – the second longest in the world.

The traditional architecture of Arabia is equally impressive – for example the multi-storey mud walled houses of Shibam in the Hadramaut region of Yemen ….

And throughout the region – countless beautiful mosques*.

Jumeirah Mosque, Dubai

* *See* page 23.

Climate

Arabia has a reputation as a hot and dusty place and in the summer (June to September), temperatures reach 40°C on the coast (often made worse by high humidity) and 50°C inland.

However, the worst effects of the heat are largely mitigated by universal air-conditioning in homes, cars, offices and shops.

Spring and autumn can be most agreeable

with pleasant temperatures and cool breezes. Winters can be surprisingly cold, particularly inland. Finally, rain is rare except in parts of Asir, Yemen and Oman*.

* *See* Country Annexes on page 89 for further details of climate.

2

Heritage

Arabia's culture is rooted in a rich and proud heritage . . .

. . . of ancient civilisations, birthplace of the world's third great monotheistic faith – Islam, the Arabic language, a huge Arab empire, the tribal Bedu tradition, and in modern times, the establishment of independent nation states.

Ancient Civilizations

In ancient history Arabia was home to a succession of cultures which emerged as a result of the seafaring contacts between Mesopotamia (Iraq) and the Indus Valley (Pakistan and India) and trade with the Levant, Rome and Greece in the valuable products of the region – pearls from the Gulf and copper, gold and frankincense from southern Arabia. Frankincense, an aromatic gum from trees that grow only in Oman, Yemen and Somalia, was a particularly valuable commodity used in religious rites.

However, these civilisations were mainly confined to the coastal regions and Southern Arabia, leaving the vast desert interior isolated – the harsh terrain proving an effective deterrent to invader and coloniser alike.

The Bedu Tradition

This isolation continued in most parts of the Arabian interior right up to the second half of the twentieth century and guaranteed a remarkable continuity of the ancient ways – in particular the customs and traditions of the nomadic Bedu (*sing*. Bedouin).

The Bedu way of life, although now fast disappearing, was superbly adapted to the harsh and often dangerous environment in which they lived, tending their flocks of sheep and goats and supported by their lifeline, the camel. They were hardy, proud and fiercely independent and considered themselves markedly superior to settled folk in villages and towns – although each had need of the other.

The basis of Bedu society was the tribe. It dominated a territorial area, usually designated by pasture and water wells, and was made up of clans consisting of a number of families.

The tribe was led by a shaikh* – elected by consensus – not automatically passed from father to son but always remaining within the same family. Each member of the tribe had direct right of access to the shaikh and could converse with him on an equal footing addressing him by name and without honorific title. Although the word of the shaikh was law he was expected to consult the elders of the tribe, especially on matters affecting the tribe as a whole.

Tribal society was governed by a strict and time-honoured code of conduct, with set procedures for the settlement of disputes and the punishment of crimes. Deference was always shown to the elders, the poor were cared for and above all was the inviolable rule of hospitality.

On an individual level, a Bedouin's word was his bond and his loyalty to family and tribe unswerving – values which in spite of the transition to a modern lifestyle, remain at the heart of Arabian culture today**.

* Pronounced 'shake' and not 'chic'.

** *See* Chapter 6 – Modern Society.

The Birth of Islam

The most important event in the history of Arabia took place in Makkah (also written Mecca) in the year AD 622 – the birth of the world's third and last great Semitic monotheistic religion – Islam.

The gradual revelation of Islam to the Prophet Muhammad is described in detail in the next chapter but by the time of his death in AD 632 the faith had spread widely throughout Arabia.

The Prophet's successors, the Caliphs, then continued this expansion through conquest and by AD 750 had established a huge empire extending from Spain to the frontiers of China.

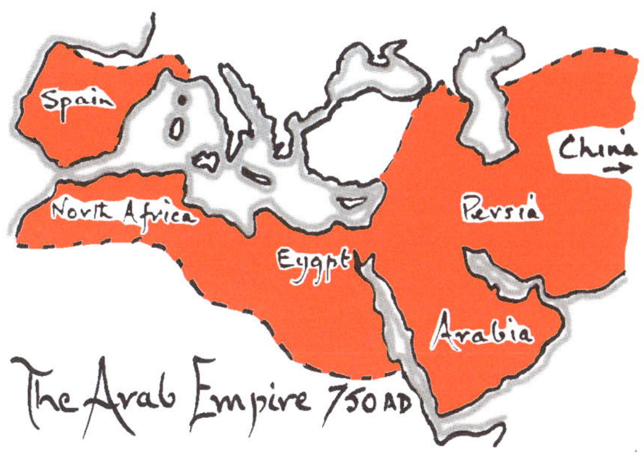

At this time the Arabs were at the forefront of learning, keeping alive the ancient Greek scholarship and subsequently passing it on to Western Europe – and adding much that was new in medicine, astronomy and science*.

> "No people in the early Middle Ages contributed to human progress so much as did the Arabs – Arab scholars were studying Aristotle when Charlemagne and his lords were reportedly learning to write their names. Scientists in Cordova, with their seventeen great libraries, each of which included more than 400,000 volumes, enjoyed luxurious baths at a time when washing the body was considered a dangerous custom at the University of Oxford."
> Professor Phillip Hitti, *The Arabs – A Short History*

This contribution to Western learning is amply evidenced by the numerous Arabic words in the English language – alchemy, alcohol, algebra, admiral, arsenal, etc. Our star names – Rigel, Betelgeuse etc., are largely Arabic.

* The Arabs introduced the numerals 1 to 9 that we use today.

However, the power base of the Arab conquests under the Caliphate moved away from Arabia, first to Damascus and then to Baghdad and Arabia's role in the empire became less significant – except for the annual pilgrimage to Makkah which continued, as it has done ever since – uninterrupted for more than 1,300 years.

The isolation of Arabia from foreign influence was briefly challenged in the sixteenth century by the Portuguese and the Ottoman Turks. Portuguese interest was limited to securing their sea routes to Asia and they built a series of forts along the Arabian and Gulf coast at such places as Muscat, Bahrain and Tarut*, many of which can still be seen today.

Fort Jalali - Oman

The Ottoman Turks on the other hand, conquered Yemen and brought the holy cities of Makkah and Madinah under their control and penetrated the Gulf as far as Bahrain and Al-Hasa until the Ottoman Empire finally collapsed during the First World War.

* *See* map on page 98.

The last foreign power to wield direct influence in the region was the British in the nineteenth and twentieth centuries, mainly, like the Portuguese before them, in connection with their interests further east – primarily in India. The colonisation of Aden and treaties with rulers in the Gulf were all directed to this end.

However, by 1972 all the territories of Arabia had become independent nation states*.

In the last forty years the politics and economics of Arabia have been transformed with the exploitation of the region's vast oil resources, the acquisition of enormous wealth, the establishment of modern infrastructures and cities and a lightning transition into the technological age.

'By God!'

* *See* Country Annexes on page 89.

3

Islam

Islam is all pervasive in Arabia and, without some understanding of it, life there will be incomprehensible. Its teachings govern a Muslim's complete way of life.

Translated from the Arabic, Islam means 'submission' (to the will of God) and a Muslim* is 'one who has submitted to God'. A Muslim's faith is intense and his submission to God, absolute.

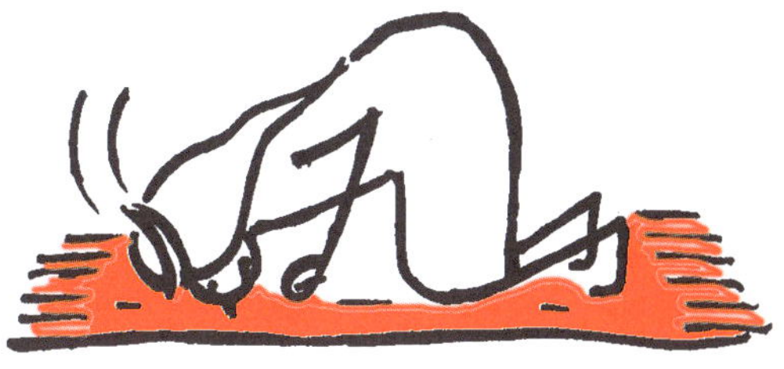

* It is important to pronounce the 's' of the word Muslim as the smooth 's' of 'slim' and not as the hard 's' of 'chisel' which has another, and offensive, meaning.

The Muslim word for God is ***al**lah* and a Muslim's creed is expressed in the brief statement:

__ash__hadu al-laa il__laah__a illa __al__lah, wa __ash__hadu
anna mu__ham__madan ra__sool__ al__lah__!

I testify that (there is) no god but the God and I testify that Muhammad (is the) Messenger of God!

This creed is based on the Oneness and Uniqueness of God, that Islam was revealed as the direct word of God to the last of His Prophets, Muhammad (PBUH*), that this was the last of God's revelations and is recorded for all time in the Holy Quran – in the Arabic language.

The Prophet Muhammad

The Prophet Muhammad was born in AD 570 in Makkah, in present day Saudi Arabia. He was a member of the influential Quraysh tribe.

In AD 610 at the age of 40, Muhammad received his first revelation from God through the Archangel Gabriel and as more revelations followed he gradually became aware that he had been chosen as the Messenger of God. He began to preach his message but was at first scorned and persecuted and in AD 622 he and his followers were obliged to flee to Madinah**.

* When mentioning the Prophet Muhammad, Muslims often add 'peace be upon him' or, in writing, PBUH.
** Also in Saudi Arabia north of Makkah. *See* map on page 98.

The Flight

The date of this flight, the *hijra* (lit. 'migration' in Arabic) is the official start of the Islamic era – Anno Hijra or AH (*see* page 24).

Following the flight, however, the Prophet began to win significant recognition and in AD 630 returned victorious to Makkah. By the time of his death in AD 632, Islam had been accepted throughout Arabia. Makkah and Madinah are the two holiest places in Islam.

The Prophet's successors, the Caliphs (from the Arabic word *khaleefa* meaning 'successor'), continued the expansion of the faith through conquest and establishing, as explained in Chapter 2, an immense Arab empire.

The newcomer to the Muslim world will hear of groupings within Islam, in particular the Sunni and the Shi'a. These originate in a disagreement which arose after the death of the Prophet over the succession to the Caliphate, between those who favoured an elected Caliph and chose Abu Bakr, the Prophet's closest companion and father-in-law, as the first Caliph and those who considered it should remain in the Prophet's family and be his cousin and son-in-law, Ali. The former group became known as Sunni from the Arabic word ***sunna*** meaning 'customary or orthodox procedure' and the latter as Shi'a, from the Arabic *shi'at ali* meaning 'Party of Ali'.

This disagreement swiftly led to the split between the two groups when Ali, who eventually became Caliph, was assassinated and his son Hussain was later martyred in Shi'a eyes, in an attempt to win back the Caliphate. The Shi'a revere the memory of Ali and Hussain.

The large majority of the world's 800 million Muslims are Sunni but the Shi'a are the predominant group in Iran and comprise a majority of the population in Iraq and Bahrain. There are also significant Shi'a minorities in Kuwait, UAE, Yemen and the Eastern Province of Saudi Arabia and numbers in most other Arab countries.

The doctrines of the Shi'a do not differ greatly from those of the Sunni although Shi'a emphasise the spiritual authority of their *imams* (from the Arabic 'he who goes before'), who lead Muslims in prayer, and of certain others in the Islamic hierarchy.

It would be wrong to attach too much importance to this division. As one might expect in a religion of so many adherents, different schools of thought have also emerged within the Sunni and Shi'a groupings themselves – notably, as far as the Peninsula is concerned, the Muwahhidoon, a Sunni group predominant in Saudi Arabia, and the Zaidis, a Shi'a group with a significant presence in Yemen. A further, independent group, the Ibadhis, are predominant in Oman.

The Holy Quran

The revelation of God's message to the Prophet Muhammad is written down in the Quran* (also spelt Koran) and set out in 114 *sura* (chapters).

To a Muslim, the Quran is the infallible word of God and treated with the utmost reverence and because God chose to make His revelation in Arabic, the language itself has a sacred quality for Muslims. They find its power of expression deeply moving. The Arabic of the Quran is regarded as the standard for classical Arabic which is in turn the basis for the written language used throughout the Arab world.

The Quran is the primary source of the revealed Islamic law known as the ***shari'a***. It is supplemented by the ***hadeeth*** – the recorded sayings and deeds of the Prophet and the ***sunna*** – the practice, of the Prophet.

The Quran occupies an even more important place in Islam than that of the Bible in Christianity. The Quran prescribes exact directions for every aspect of a Muslim's life – not only for worship but also for marriage, divorce, honourable behaviour, actions towards the poor, punishment for crimes and even economic activity.

* Lit. 'recitation' in Arabic. The Quran is greatly revered in Islam and a non-Muslim should avoid handling a copy in the presence of a Muslim without permission.

The Five Pillars of Islam

These are the five obligatory acts required of every Muslim:

- The Declaration of Faith
- Prayer
- Almsgiving
- Fasting
- The Pilgrimage to Makkah

1

The Declaration of Faith – *sha**haa**da* (lit. 'bearing witness') testifies to the unity of God and that Muhammad is his Prophet:

***ash**hadu al-laa il**laa**ha illa **al**lah, wa **ash**hadu anna mu**ham**madan ra**sool** al**lah**!*
I testify that (there is) no god but the God and I testify that Muhammad (is the) Messenger of God!

2

Prayer – *sa**lah***. Observance of the five daily prayers at dawn, noon, afternoon, sunset and evening and the Friday noon-day prayers in the mosque. Prior to prayer a Muslim washes his hands, face and feet. He prays in the direction of Makkah.

Alms tax – *zakat*. Muslims have a duty to pay *zakat* each year to help the poor. This is a set portion of their wealth and these days is usually paid in money rather than in kind.

Fasting – *sawm* (pr. soam). Each year throughout the holy month of Ramadan, the ninth month of the Islamic calendar*, Muslims observe a fast and are required to abstain from food, drink, smoking and all pleasurable pursuits between sunrise and sunset. Ramadan ends with the festival of *eed al-fitr***.

The pilgrimage to Makkah – *hajj*. It is obligatory for every Muslim, once in his lifetime, provided he can afford it and his health allows, to make the pilgrimage to Makkah and the other holy places of Islam. This takes place during the twelfth month of the Islamic year and for it the Muslim exchanges his normal dress for two plain sheets of white cloth.

* *See* page 24.
** *See* page 52.

The Pilgrimage

During the pilgrimage the pilgrim will:

- Firstly, circle the ***ka**'ba** situated in the Grand Mosque in Makkah – seven times.
- Move outside the city and journey seven times between two small hills, acting out the frantic search of Abraham's wife Hagar hunting for water for her son, Ishmael.
- Stand and meditate at the Mount of Mercy in the Plain of Arafat from midday to sunset.
- Then go to Mina, near Makkah, carry out the stoning of the three pillars which symbolise the temptations of Satan and perform the sacrifice of an animal.

The pilgrimage ends with the most important festival in the Muslim calendar – *eed al-**ad**ha* (the feast of the sacrifice). Traditionally, a sheep, goat or other acceptable animal is slaughtered in commemoration of Abraham's sacrifice of the ram in place of his son.

A man who has performed the pilgrimage is privileged to call himself and be addressed as *al-haajj* (the pilgrim) or less formally ***ha**jji*. Similarly a woman would be addressed as *al-**haa**jja* or *ha**jji**a* (the final 'a' being the feminine ending of words in Arabic).

* *See* illustration on page 53.

The Mosque

The classic features of a mosque (***mas**jid*) are a rectangular courtyard (*saha*) with a fountain or washroom for the obligatory ablutions (*wudu*), a prayer hall (*sa**jaa**da* or *mu**salla***), often with a domed roof, a niche (***mih**raab*) indicating the direction (***qib**la*) of the Grand Mosque in Makkah* and beside it a pulpit (***min**bar*) from which the leader of the prayers preaches the Friday sermon. Lastly, a minaret (*mi**naa**ra*) from which the Muezzin (*mu'**adhdh**in*) calls the faithful to prayer, these days by loud speaker.

Prayers do not have to be said in a mosque. Muslims pray wherever they happen to be at the time of prayer. This may be in an office or in the open. Don't be surprised when you first see it. In Arabia it is a common everyday sight. If someone is praying in public, one should avoid walking immediately in front of them.

* *See* also Saudi Arabia Annex on page 99.

The Islamic Calendar

The Islamic Hejirian calendar is based on twelve lunar months and this is used for all religious purposes. The lunar months are shorter than those in the Gregorian calendar and overall the Hejirian year is shorter than the Gregorian by some eleven days. Hence the date of each Islamic festival advances eleven days or so in each Gregorian year.

The principal annual Muslim festivals are:

- *lailat al-**mi**'raj* – the Prophet's night journey to heaven via Jerusalem.
- *sawm ramadhaan* – The Holy Fast of Ramadan.
- *eed al-fitr* – the festival end of the fast of Ramadan.
- *eed al-**adha*** – The Feast of Sacrifice at the end of the annual Pilgrimage.
- *ras as-sana* – the Muslim New Year.
- ***ashura*** – Shi'a day of remembrance on the anniversary of the martyrdom of Hussain.*
- ***maw**lid an-nabi* – The Prophet Muhammad's birthday.

The exact date of each festival depends on the sighting of the moon and may vary by a day or two from place to place.

* *See* Pages 17 and 18.

The Working Week

The working week in Arabia is either from Sunday to Thursday (in the Gulf countries) or from Saturday to Wednesday (in Saudi Arabia). Friday is the holy day set aside for communal worship in the mosque and it is the greatest *faux pas* for a Westerner to contact a Muslim in the Arab world on business on a Friday.

The daily routine in the region, particularly during the summer months, is to work from quite early in the morning until early afternoon, break for a siesta at lunchtime and resume work for a few hours in the late afternoon or evening. Government offices are usually only open in the first half of the day. These hours are often extended in winter. During the fast of Ramadan working hours are severely curtailed particularly towards the end of the month and shop opening hours become erratic.

The importance of his faith to a Muslim cannot be overstated. His everyday speech is full of references to God. There are dozens – even hundreds – of expressions in the Arabic language which invoke the name of ***allah***. Perhaps the best known is *in-**sha**'allah* which means 'if God wills (it)' a phrase frequently added to any expression of future intent. This is not just a formulaic religious sentiment – to a Muslim, it is a necessary qualification in view of his firm belief that everything that happens on earth is ordained by God.

'If God wills'

4

Language, Literature and Art

Arabic is a fascinating and beautiful language. Originating in northern Arabia, it is now spoken throughout the Arab world by over 300 million people and is the religious language of a further 1.2 billion Muslims in 150 other countries.

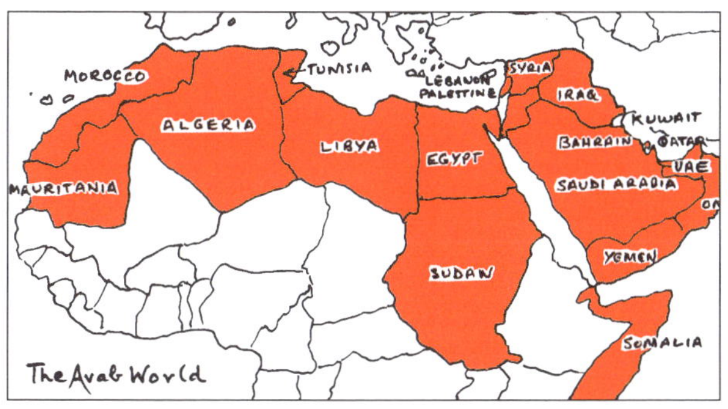

It is the official language of all the Arabian countries although English is also widely used.

N.B. The word 'Arabic' should only be used to describe the language. 'Arab' on the other hand, a noun and an adjective, can refer to 'an Arab' or anything Arab, *e.g.* 'Arab customs'.

A concentrated course of instruction is necessary to learn to speak Arabic with any degree of fluency and most visitors to Arabia do not have the time or indeed the requirement to learn it since English is widely spoken. However, it is certainly interesting to understand something of the structure of the language and a knowledge of the basic courtesies will earn one a disproportionate amount of kudos and appreciation . . .

As mentioned in Chapter 3, because God's revelation to the Prophet Muhammad, enshrined in the Quran, was in Arabic, the language has a sacred quality for Muslims and is revered as the 'language of God'.

Classical Arabic is rich in vocabulary, breadth of meaning, hyperbole, metaphor, rhyme and rhythm. When recited from the Quran – or in poetry or prose – in its purest form, the literary eloquence and power of expression excites the senses of the Arab listener in a way that has to be seen to be believed. They find it intensely moving.

Written or literary Arabic is based on the classical language and is the same throughout the Arab world. This is the language used in newspapers, books, public notices and in radio and television broadcasts. Spoken Arabic, on the other hand, varies – each country or region having its own dialect. In Arabia, fortunately, these differences in speech are not marked.

Arabic is a Semitic language like Hebrew and Aramaic (the language of Jesus) which belong to a totally different family to European languages. Arabic is structurally different from English but in many ways is easier to learn and the grammar more logical in that its rules are obeyed, whereas English seems full of exceptions.

In common with all Semitic languages, a major feature of Arabic is that most words are based on a three letter verbal root from which all words connected with the area of meaning of that root are formed. Thus from the verbal root **k-t-b** meaning 'to write' come *kit**aab*** (a book), ***kaa**tib* (a clerk), ***mak**tab* (an office) and ***mak**taba* (a library or bookshop).

The Arabic script is written from right to left and has an alphabet of 28 consonants, three long vowels and three short ones – the latter not normally written – the logic of the language making it unnecessary.

The script is cursive in that most of the letters can be joined together. There are no capital letters and unlike English there is no basic difference between the handwritten and printed form of the language.

Arabic is a phonetic language, i.e. it is pronounced exactly as it is written – unlike English which has many silent letters, viz the ‘h’ and ‘u’ in ‘honour’.

The only apparent complication of the script is that the letters change their shape depending on whether they come at the beginning, middle or end of a word but this system is entirely logical in that each letter has a unique characteristic which makes it clearly recognisable wherever it appears in a word. For example the first three letters of the Arabic alphabet are:

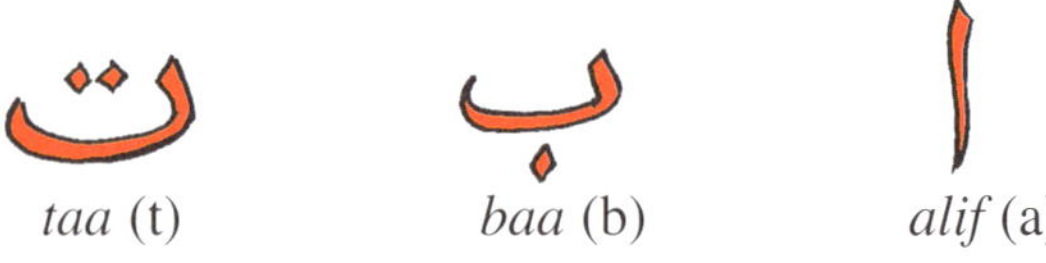

taa (t) *baa* (b) *alif* (a)

Written from right to left

Written at the beginning of a word they appear:

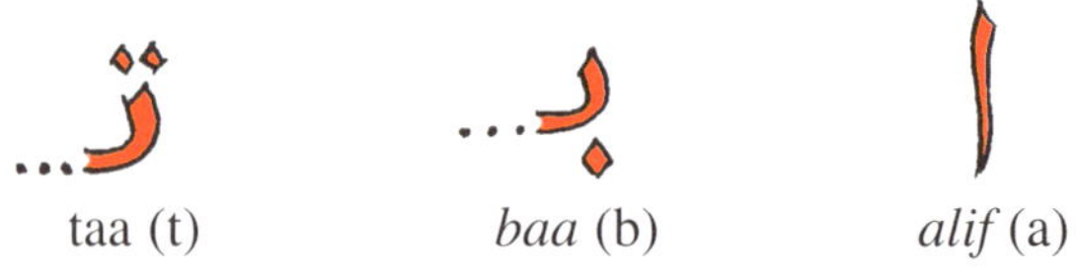

taa (t) *baa* (b) *alif* (a)

Written in the middle of a word:

taa (t) *baa* (b) *alif* (a)

And at the end of a word they are written:

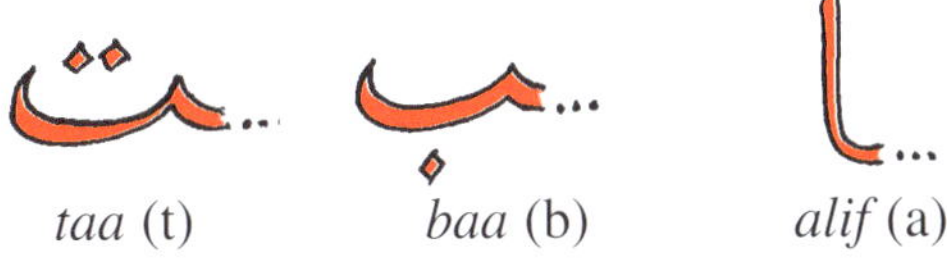

taa (t) *baa* (b) *alif* (a)

One can see that the main characteristic of each letter is retained – the vertical line in the case of the *alif* (or 'a') – the dot below the letter in the case of the *baa* (or 'b') and the two dots above the letter in the case of the *taa* (or 't')*.

Although English is widely spoken in Arabia and many Arabs speak it fluently, some do not and it is always best to use straightforward English and avoid the vernacular. Expressions such as 'state of the art' for example may well not be understood. And when a customs official says 'Give passport!' he is not necessarily being rude. Those may well be the only words he knows in English.

* For those wishing to look further into the Arabic language and script, the two sister volumes to this book – *Very Simple Arabic* and *Very Simple Arabic Script* are intended to provide a simple introduction.

Literature

Historically, the Arabs have expressed their artistic nature through the spoken word – the highest form of which was poetry. The poet was held in the highest regard in Arab society. He was their oracle, orator (in war and peace), spokesman and historian. Together with prose, poetry was committed to memory and passed down by word of mouth from generation to generation. The themes of the early poems were of nomadic life, love stories, battles, acts of heroism and satires. This love of poetry and the esteem in which a poet is held exists to this day.

Arab literature today is dominated by the writings of the Quran which is neither prose nor poetry but is universally considered by Muslims to be a work of unsurpassable excellence. The appeal of the language when recited from the Quran is a unique feature of Arabic and although translated into numerous other languages for the benefit of the many non-Arab Muslims in the world, its true meaning and quality can only be appreciated in the original Arabic.

The Quran is interpreted as forbidding the portrayal of the human form, at least in decorating religious buildings. This explains the almost total absence of naturalistic and representational art in the Arab world which is so prominent in other cultures.

Arabesque

As a result, artistic style in the Muslim world has developed around decorative floral and geometric forms which have evolved into the characteristic interwoven recurrent motifs of the design known as Arabesque.

Arabesque

For the same reason Arabic script, particularly of religious texts, gave rise to the foremost of the Islamic decorative arts – calligraphy.

Calligraphy

Decorative calligraphic inscription is seen everywhere in the Arab world – in beautifully decorated mosques, architectural monuments, pottery, glassware and most of all in the countless handwritten copies of the Quran itself.

Modern Islamic art continues the ancient tradition of compositions based on extracts from the Quran in a variety of designs including birds and animals . . .

Calligraphy of religious texts is commonly used in decorating greetings cards for the religious festivals.

Modern Arab institutions make use of calligraphy in producing attractive logos:

Logo of the Dubai airline Emirates

Traditional arts and crafts in the Arab world include the production of beautiful gold and silver ornaments and jewellery, ceramics, copper and brassware, flat weave rugs (*kelim*), exquisite fine needlework, swords and silver daggers, wood carving and embroidered dresses.

Omani silver ***khanjar*** (dagger)

(The Omani ***khanjar*** appears on the flag of Oman as part of the National Emblem)

Architecture

Traditional buildings use local materials – clay, stone and gypsum and, with the notable exception of the tower houses of Yemen*, the brightly painted houses in Asir and the elegant coral houses of the Red Sea coast, tend to be plain and unadorned like this restored old Dubai house with its wind-towers.

Bastakia Courtyard - Dubai

Modern buildings on the other hand, often reflect the traditions and culture of the region such as this beautiful golf clubhouse in Dubai.

Dubai Creek Golf and Yacht Club

**See* page 5.

5

Etiquette

Good manners are considered extremely important in Arabia and there is a strict code of social conduct or etiquette. A foreigner must know something about it if he or she wishes to get on with Arabs.

The first thing likely to impress you about the Arab is his unfailing hospitality . . .

***bay**tee **bay**tak!*
'My house is your house!'

. . . and you should of course reciprocate when the occasion arises.

On Meeting An Arab

Always shake hands*. An Arab may well keep hold of your hand while talking to you after shaking hands. This is a perfectly normal custom and a mark of friendship.

The basic pleasantries in Arabic are given below and if the foreigner takes the trouble to learn them he can be sure of an enthusiastic reception.

*An exception to this rule is that it is not normal for a man to shake the hand of an Arab woman unless she follows the Western custom and specifically offers it.

The reply *al-**ham**doolil**lah** bi-**khair*** or more often simply *al-**ham**doolil**lah***, – lit. 'Praise be to God' means 'I am well' and it is customary always to give this reply. In this the Muslim is acknowledging God's will over all things.

* This may be used at any time.
** *kayf **haa**lik?* to a woman. The reply is the same.

Good Morning

Greeting

Reply

Good Afternoon or Good Evening

Greeting

Reply

* Less formal greeting sometimes used which strictly means 'Welcome'. Exceptionally, the *u* in *mur**huba*** is pronounced as the 'u' in 'but'. *murhuba**tayn*** means 'two *mur**huba**s*'.

** ***bee**kum* if replying to more than one person and ***bee**kee* if replying to a woman.

Goodbye

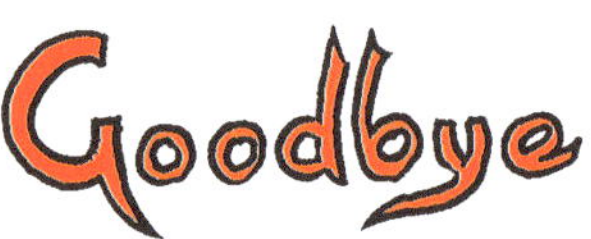

The two main variations for 'Goodbye' are:

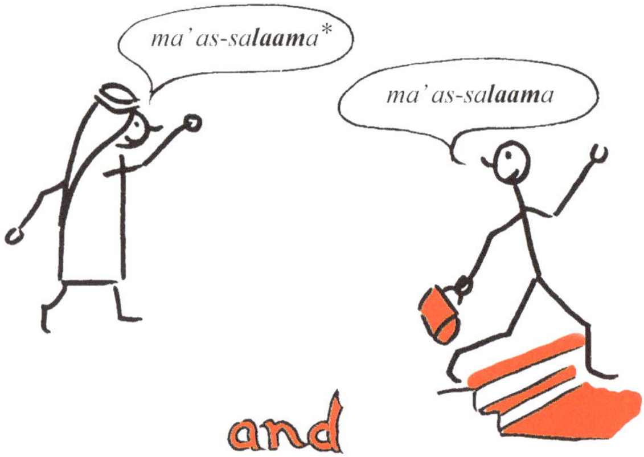
ma' as-salaama*
ma' as-salaama

and

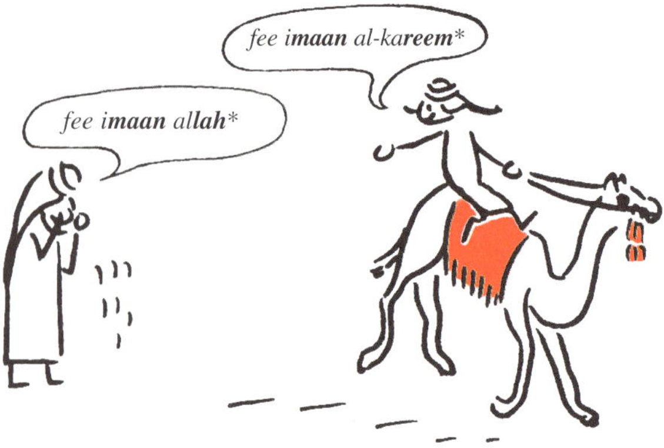
fee imaan al-kareem*
fee imaan allah*

You may also hear *fee **imaan** a**llah*** and *fee* *wi**daa'at** a**llah*** in reply.

* *See* translations in the Glossary on page 104.

You Pay A Call

After shaking hands and exchanging greetings the person on whom you call will ask you to sit down . . .

Your host will indicate a seat. The most important visitor usually sits in the closest seat on the host's right hand.

Don't be surprised if someone gets up to make way for you. It means you are considered more important – for the moment anyway.

Do not sit in such a way that the sole of your foot is presented to another person. This used to mean, and still does to a certain extent, that you are intentionally insulting that person – since the sole of the foot is unclean. It is therefore best not to cross your legs.

After initial greetings, enquiries are invariably made into each other's health – a formula observed no matter how frequently you meet someone or talk on the phone. Your host may then initiate talk on general topics such as your journey, whether you have visited the region before, your first impressions, the weather etc.

When you get to know an Arab well you might also enquire into the wellbeing of his collective family and children but because of the greater privacy accorded to women in the Arab world, never specifically of his wife.

What happens next depends on your host. He may or may not follow the custom of offering you refreshment before raising the purpose of your visit. It is increasingly the case in business circles to dispense with some of these formalities.

If however, your host abides by the old customs a servant will offer coffee or tea. Arab coffee is pale, bitter and often flavoured with cardamom and other spices. It is traditionally served by pouring a small quantity for each guest into a small round cup.

Take the cup in the right hand. The right hand only is used when drinking, eating, smoking and offering anything.

Smoking a hookah – in Arabic a *nargeela* or ***sheesha***.

It is customary to drink at least one cup or you risk offending your host but not more than three. The signal you use to show that you have had enough is to give the empty cup a quick twist as you hand it back.

Tea in Arabia can be served sweet or bitter but without milk in a small glass cup and saucer.

These are the most common refreshments in Arabia but one may also be offered instant coffee or tea with milk and sugar in the Western style or even Turkish coffee (sweet, medium or plain without sugar) served with a glass of water which is drunk first. Turkish coffee should be sipped until an inch of liquid remains in the cup or you risk swallowing the thick coffee grounds.

It may now be opportune to mention the subject of your visit but it is always best to be patient and take the lead from your host.

The hospitality of some Arabs is such that they keep 'open office', *i.e.* visitors are free to enter at any time. Indeed, you may, as a businessman, enter the office of a potential client to find other businessmen present. In this case, announce yourself, exchange pleasantries, accept refreshments and when asked your business give enough information to interest your host in granting you an exclusive meeting at a later date.

One of the major hurdles for a foreigner in understanding the culture of Arabia is the Arab perception of time. It is quite different from that in the West. Always be on time for an appointment but be prepared for it to be delayed, often for a considerable period, or even postponed. This is not inefficiency or bad manners but the result of a totally different attitude to life which is lived to different criteria and at a different pace. The reason for delay may be perfectly valid in the Arab culture and one must accept it with equanimity and never evidence any annoyance. For this reason alone it is inadvisable to work to a tight schedule in Arabia.

Forms of address are important. An Arab is formally called ***say**yid* (Mr) or ***say**yida* (Mrs) followed by the given and other names* but in conversation it is usual to address them by their first name only. A ruling shaikh is 'Your Highness' initially and 'Sir' thereafter and other shaikhs, government ministers and ambassadors are 'Your Excellency'.

* *See* explanation of Arab names on page 69.

When calling to an Arab it is polite to prefix his name with *ya* …

Remembering Arab names* can be difficult but it is important to get them right. Most Arabs have printed cards in English and Arabic. It may help to have your own card printed in the same way.

And finally, do not call at siesta time …

* *See* explanation of Arab Names on page 69.

A Hafla

The Arabic word for a party is ***hafla***. You may be fortunate enough to receive an invitation.

If the party is in a private Arab house it will normally be an all-male or all-female occasion. You might take a small gift but it is not usually appropriate for a male guest to take flowers for a host's wife although it would be if the guest was a woman. It is best to seek local advice.

When you hand a gift to an Arab friend do not be surprised if he does not open it or even thank you. This is the normal custom in Arabia however difficult it is for Westerners to understand. Your friend may also start to refuse the gift, indicating that you should not have taken the trouble but you should politely insist it be accepted.

The time of your arrival will vary depending on the type and circumstances of the party and who the host is. It is sometimes correct to arrive exactly on time and at others to delay for five or six minutes or even longer. It is best to seek advice…

On arrival, it is customary to remove your shoes. Greet the elders first and sit in the seat offered you. Dinner is traditionally eaten late. Expect a lot of talk beforehand but not during the meal itself.

Eating may well take place at floor level in which case again, avoid presenting the soles of your feet to anyone and use only your right hand.

Immediately after the meal it is customary to thank your host with the words ***sufra da'ima*** which means 'May your table always be spread'. Coffee is then served, soon after which you should take your leave …

You may also wish to entertain. If it is a formal occasion such as reception in a hotel, you should ideally issue an invitation in Arabic. Any local printer will help you. Do not attempt to mimic all the Arab customs – English food is quite acceptable except that a Muslim is forbidden by the laws of Islam to eat pork or drink alcohol. A buffet supper might have a discreet notice saying that the food does not contain any pork products.

Eeds

The Arabic word for a festival is *eed*. There are a number of important religious festivals each year* the exact dates of which change in our Gregorian calendar because the Islamic Calendar (Hejirian) is based on the lunar cycle **.

You need only concern yourself with the two main festivals…

The largest is *eed al-**adha*** and is celebrated at the end of the pilgrimage to Makkah. As explained in Chapter 3, a major feature of the pilgrimage is the circumambulation of the ***ka'ba***, the cube shaped building in the Grand Mosque in Makkah which holds the famous Black Stone, sacred to all Muslims.

* *See* list on page 24.
** *See* explanation on page 24.

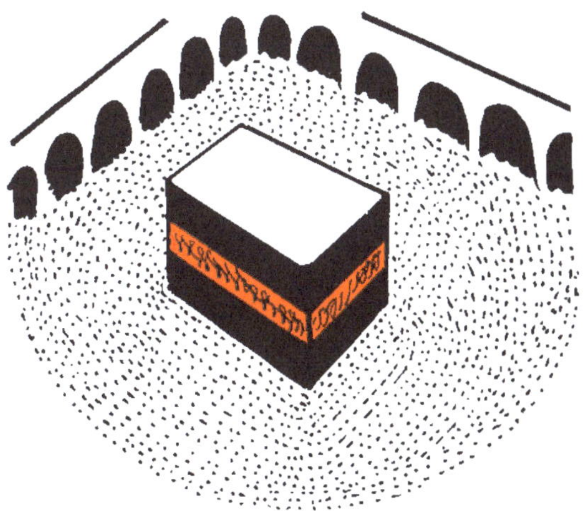

The ***ka'ba*** in the Grand Mosque in Makkah

The other main festival is the *eed al-fitr** (pr. 'fitter'), which takes place at the end of the fast of Ramadan.

Ramadan lasts for a full lunar month. All Muslims are required to abstain from food, drink and tobacco and all other pleasurable pursuits between sunrise and sunset.

This can be a great burden especially if the month of fasting falls in the heat of the summer. Working hours are significantly curtailed.

Naturally, you should show consideration and not eat, drink or smoke in the presence of a Muslim during daylight hours in Ramadan. In any case, you will probably find it is a punishable offence to do so in most Arabian countries. In addition a Western woman should dress soberly during Ramadan, *i.e.* she should not wear a short skirt or sleeveless top.

Ramadan ends with a feast …

When you meet a Muslim on the day of either festival or in the days closely following them you should shake hands and congratulate them using a special greeting …

* Congratulations on the *eed*! *See* Glossary on page 104

** Alternatively you may hear *ayaamak saeeda*.

There is a public holiday of between four days and a week on the occasion of each *eed* and greetings cards are usually sent to friends, important officials and business clients (to arrive a day or two in advance of the *eed*). The cards are available from Arab stationery shops and printers and look like this …

Some large institutions and companies have their own cards specially printed incorporating their logo. You should not forget to sign the card.

You will sometimes receive a card of thanks in reply which will look like this …

أشكركم على تهانيكم بالعيد السعيد
وكل عام وأنتم بخير

It is customary to give house servants a gift of money on the occasion of each *eed*.

It is also the custom at both festivals for important people to hold open audiences in their palaces or homes and this offers a good opportunity for a foreigner to meet them and pay their respects. You should enter the house, greet the important individual and others you judge to be important, particularly the elders, congratulating them on the *eed*. You then take a seat, accept refreshment and after a suitable interval take your leave.

Arab families and friends visit each other at *eed* time and a visiting foreigner would be equally welcome to call.

You may also give a small present to the children of an Arab family if you visit one …

Miscellaneous Points

The first problem you face in Arabia may be the heat. It can make people who are not used to it tired and perhaps short tempered.

The laws concerning alcohol and particularly drugs* are strictly enforced in some Arab countries where the possession of even a small quantity of alcohol is punishable with imprisonment and the possession of drugs can be a capital offence . . .

You may also find a ban on certain DVDs and certainly the 'Playboy' type of magazine. Advice on all these matters can be obtained from your airline or travel agency before departure.

* *See* Country Annexes on page 89.

Taxis in Arabia do not always have meters. In this case it is wise to agree the fare in advance to avoid any nasty surprises. Tipping taxi drivers is not expected but it is normal for porters, hotel staff and in restaurants if there is no service charge.

You will discover that the Arab sense of humour is remarkably similar to that in the West. However, avoid telling jokes until you know someone well.

In general conversation with an Arab, at least on first acquaintance, avoid discussion about religion, women and the politics of the Arab world.

Don't be surprised when offering something to an Arab – say a drink – if he says '***shukran***', *i.e.* 'thank you' but means that he is refusing. This is a customary way of saying 'No' in Arabia.

If you are unfortunate enough to be involved in a car accident in Arabia it is obligatory to stay with your vehicle until the police arrive. They assess the situation and make a report which apportions blame for judicial and insurance purposes. This report is required by any garage before it will carry out repairs. In addition, whatever the rights and wrongs of the matter keep your cool. It always pays to be calm, dignified and polite …

You should be aware that in Arabia a dog is considered unclean, except perhaps for the Saluki – the Arabian gazelle hound.

An Arab uses his hands as a means of expression as much as a Frenchman does. You may also witness the following Arab gestures …

… putting the tips of the fingers and thumb together and moving the hand up and down to mean 'Patience!', 'Patience!' …

… putting the fingers of the right hand together pointing downwards and pulling the hand towards them when beckoning someone …

… one should never beckon with one finger in the Western way as this has an offensive connotation in the Arab world …

* 'Come!'

… and pulling the point of one's chin to mean …

'Shame on you!'

Sooner or later you will experience a variation to the customary handshake. If his hands are dirty or wet, an Arab will offer you his right wrist which you should shake in the normal way.

Care should be taken when translating from English into Arabic. It is possible to render an English word or phrase directly into Arabic and for the result to be meaningless or even offensive.

Certain mosques in Arabia are open to non-Muslims visitors who should dress conservatively – men should not wear shorts* or sleeveless shirts and women should wear long sleeves and a reasonable length skirt. On entering a mosque visitors must remove their shoes, wear slippers if provided and women must wear a headscarf.

For both cultural and security reasons cameras should be used with care in Arabia. Visitors should only photograph obvious tourist sites, ask permission before photographing people and avoid photographing women.

Do not admire anything belonging to an Arab or by their custom they may feel obliged to make you a gift of it! Even if you succeed in refusing it may take a long time.

Finally, here are some common words not previously mentioned that you may find useful …

'Please'

* In Arabia it is frowned upon to wear shorts in public.

'Thank you'

'Be pleased to …'

… when offering a seat, coffee, food etc.

'Sorry!' *(or muta'assif)*　　'Don't mention it'

* Other words are *mashkoor* and *ashkurak*.

'Good!'

'Yes!'

'No!'

* You will also hear ***ai**wa* - the other word for 'Yes'.

6

Modern Society

Modern Arabia, and the oil states in particular, is a land of contrast. Against the backdrop of a clear blue sky, shimmering sands or sea, with palm trees, camels and dhows, are modern cities, dual carriageways, skyscrapers, shopping malls and every other facet of modern life. Even in the older towns and cities the buildings, shops, transport and people display an intriguing mixture of old and new.

Over the last forty years, oil wealth has enabled Saudi Arabia and the Gulf countries to make a rapid transition from desert kingdoms to modern states*.

Family Life

However, despite the influence of modern facilities and consumer products, the culture of these countries retains its own distinct Arabian character. This is rooted in the traditions, values, customs, and etiquette of the region – family, tribe, the Arabic language and most of all, Islam.

Family is the basis of Arabian society. Even in an increasingly urban life style, the importance placed on loyalty to family, extended family, and tribe continues to dominate – grandparents, parents and children commonly living together under the same roof. Men and women have separate quarters and a non-family male visitor to an Arab home would not normally meet the womenfolk. They nevertheless exert considerable influence behind the scenes. Islam permits four wives although most Arabs today have only one. If a man does have more than one wife then the Quran directs that they must all be treated exactly the same.

* An outline description of each of the Peninsula countries is given in the Country Annexes on page 89.

Values

The traditional Arabian values of honourable behaviour, courtesy and unfailing hospitality still pertain.

On a personal level Arabs are proud and dignified - status, appearances and influence matter. Although modest, they do not admire someone who fails to exercise their authority or is self-deprecating. They are nevertheless sensitive and personal remarks about their honour, family or faith, however light hearted, may well cause offence. They are equally sensitive to any superiority of manner or behaviour which could be interpreted, however unwittingly, as patronising – they expect to be dealt with openly and on equal terms.

Arabs tend to be demonstrative, tactile and unafraid of emotion. They shake hands with everybody all the time and may hold your hand long after shaking it as a simple demonstration of friendship. It would be considered unfriendly to withdraw it. Men are seen holding hands in public but it would be considered most improper to do so with a woman. It is also commonplace for Arabs to embrace relatives, close friends, dignitaries and members of a ruling family when they greet them and symbolically kiss them on the cheeks, forehead or nose depending on the relationship and local custom. However, a Westerner would have to know an Arab extremely well before greeting them in this way.

Personal Relationships

Arabs set great store by personal relationships. The greetings, hand shakings and enquiries into each other's health and that of their family are not just polite gestures – they are genuinely meant. However, for a Westerner, a trusting relationship in Arabia takes time to establish – months or even years – but once established means a great deal.

The establishment of a rapport is crucial in any dealings in Arabia. Achieving it depends on one's character but someone of moderate views who is well mannered, diplomatic and with an open personality is likely to succeed. Among the important qualities an Arab will look for are integrity and discretion.

Although a Western visitor, expatriate, or businessman may be fortunate enough to make some close Arab friends it would be most unusual for him or her to integrate into Arab society.

And finally, if you feel you get on well with Arabs, be careful not to overdo it. It is a mistake to become over familiar or attempt to imitate the Arab way of life. Experience shows that this can often offend. The person who gets on best in the Arab world is one who, while understanding the Arab way of life, maintains a respectful distance from it.

Arab Names

Arab names consist of three parts – a given name, the father's and possibly grandfather's name and finally, the family name which often refers to a place of origin, profession or tribe. However, it is the first name which is used in everyday contact. (This is why an Arab will often address a Westerner as Mr Peter or Mr John). Arab names vary when transliterated into English and it is best to write them the way the Arabs do themselves.

Some names sound the same but are in fact different. For example *__raa__shid* and *ra__sheed__*, *__maa__jid* and *ma__jeed__*, *__saal__im* and *sa__leem__*, Others are hyphenated such as *__ab__dul-rah__maan__*. *__ab__dul* means 'servant of' and *rah__maan__* means 'the merciful' (an attribute to God). In this case the full name is always used and never *__ab__dul* on its own.

Other prefixes are *ibn* or *bin* (in the Gulf) meaning 'son of' or *bint* meaning 'daughter of'*. A man may also be known informally as *abu* (father of) followed by the name of his eldest son *e.g. abu sa__leem__* or a woman known as *umm* (mother of) followed by the name of her eldest son *e.g. umm sa__leem__*.

Finally, *al* ('the' in Arabic) is sometimes put in front of the name of a distinguished family, *e.g. al-mak__toum__*, the ruling family of Dubai.

* Women do not take their husband's name on marriage.

Arab Dress

Most Arabian men wear a long loose robe called a *thobe* or ***dish**dasha* of fine white cotton in summer and a heavier weave in winter. It is often augmented by a black, brown or fawn-coloured cloak (*bisht*). The *bisht* of a senior citizen or member of a ruling family is trimmed with gold braid. However, in rural Yemen and Asir men commonly wear a brightly patterned sarong (***fut**ah)*, shirt and often a jacket.

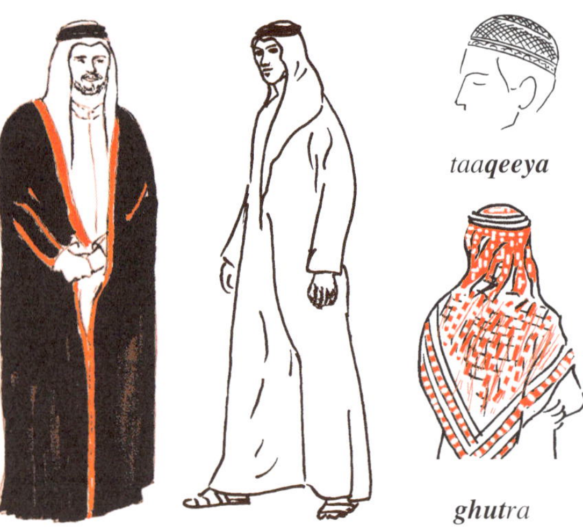

*taa**qeeya***

***ghut**ra*

In Saudi Arabia and the Gulf countries men wear a white cotton skullcap (*taa**qeeya***) and a head cloth, (***ghut**ra, ku**feeya** or she**maag***) – white, red or green cotton depending on personal choice – which is kept in place with a black rope (***'iqaal***). There are many variations of style, such as that favoured by the younger generation where the head cloth is wrapped around the head without the head rope. In addition, ardent followers of Islam will be seen wearing the patterned head cloth loosely, again without the head rope, a short thobe and a large untrimmed beard.

In Yemen and Oman the head cloth is wrapped tightly round the head or piled high like a turban. However, the most common headgear in Oman is a small round woven hat in a variety of colours and decoration, called a *kummaar*.

Yemeni headdress

An Omani *kummaar*

For a foreigner to wear traditional Arab dress is likely to cause offence and in Oman is forbidden. For similar reasons a non-Muslim foreigner should not carry prayer beads.

Arabian Women

The situation in the region with regard to women is one of the most difficult to understand – the apparent domination of men and the seclusion of women. However, it would be wrong to judge this by western standards. One is dealing with a radically different culture and moral code.

Their seclusion is a long-standing tradition and one that remains strong. As well as living in separate quarters in the family home, women pray separately from men* and a single woman is usually chaperoned by a relative in mixed company.

However, women in Arabia are not judged inferior to men. An important aspect of the Islamic faith is the protection of women's rights in such matters as ownership of property, inheritance and financial provision after divorce and as has been said, in the Arab culture, women are also extremely influential behind the scenes.

In modern Arabia women are playing an increasingly wider role in society such as in the teaching and medical professions and the media. Others are successful businesswomen and lawyers and appointed to the highest levels of government.

Arabian women traditionally wear a long black cloak (an *'a**bai**ya*), together with a headscarf and usually, but not always, a veil. Three words used variously to describe the Muslim women's veil are *hi**jaab***, the traditional Muslim headscarf, *ni**qaab***, a veil covering the whole face except for the eyes and ***bur**qa*, which in the Gulf countries refers to a rigid mask covering the nose and mouth (as opposed to the ***bur**qa* in Afghanistan – a gauze veil covering the whole face).

* Women are allotted a separate section for prayer in the mosque.

*hi**jaab***

*ni**qaab***

***bur**qa*

Foreign visitors to Arabia should of course adopt the greatest sensitivity with regard to the seclusion of Arab women and even if they are dressed in the western style, the custom of seclusion still applies. In addition, some Arab women will choose not to shake hands when being introduced to a male stranger. One should wait to see if she offers her hand before offering your own. Incidentally, the same rule applies when meeting an Arab or Muslim woman in a Western country.

Western women should dress modestly in Arabia, wearing a high neckline, long sleeves and a longish skirt. In the more conservative countries such as Saudi Arabia most also choose to wear an ***abai**ya*. When entering a mosque they should remove their shoes and wear a headscarf. Finally, they should avoid over familiarity when talking to Arab men*.

* *See* also Businesswomen on page 86.

Law and Order

Although Islamic teachings and the law enshrined in the Quran, the ***shari'a*** and the ***hadeeth**** provide the basis for every aspect of a Muslim's daily life, the needs of a modern state result in an increasing amount of secular legislation and regulation in fields such as finance, commerce, defence, health, education, social security etc. Nevertheless Islamic values are always taken into account in forming this legislation and in religious, family and social matters remain predominant. Generally speaking, Islamic values are jealously guarded as Arabian society witnesses the increase in what is seen as western influence and the demands of the contemporary state. In particular, the law-abiding characteristics of Muslim society are contrasted with the violence and degeneration seen in contemporary society in the West.

Standards of dress, laws against blasphemy and the prohibition of alcohol and drugs are strictly enforced and foreign visitors should take great care in this regard.

The countries of the region are traditionally very safe places to live. However, in the current security climate one is obliged to pay close attention to personal security and heed the advice issued by one's national government**.

* *See* page 19 ** UK citizens should visit FCO Country Profile and Travel Advice www.fco.gov.uk & US citizens www.travel.state.gov

7

Customs, Sport & Leisure

The towns and cities of modern Arabia, and the oil states in particular, boast luxury villas and hotels, ultra-modern shopping malls and facilities for every conceivable leisure activity. Arabians have embraced these benefits while retaining their traditional customs and pursuits.

Shops and supermarkets stock a range of products catering for the tastes of Arab nationals, expatriates and tourists alike – all except items that do not conform to Islamic norms – such as alcohol – although they are often available to non-Muslims in restricted outlets. The world's most fashionable brand names are widely represented.

Shopping malls incorporate restaurants and facilities for activities such as bowling, go-carting, ice skating and even (in Dubai) – skiing!

Traditional souqs, however, with their unique and timeless atmosphere remain as popular as ever. Shops selling similar merchandise are traditionally grouped together and souqs are preferred venues for buying spices, herbs, linen, perfume and particularly jewellery. Every town and city has its gold souq.

Bargaining

Bargaining is in the Arab blood. Many foreign visitors to Arabia find it tedious or else are ignorant of how to go about it. Shops may have fixed prices but in the bazaar one haggles to get the best deal.

To bargain needs time. A buyer must first establish a rapport with the seller and be prepared *not* to buy something if he considers the price too high. If he shows he is in any way keen to buy, the seller will hold out for a high price – and get it! A buyer should first decide what he is willing to pay – say X – and request the asking price. He then offers less than X but allows the seller to beat him up to it.

A vital aspect of any negotiation is to remain on good personal terms with the seller at all times. Dealings may well get heated but if there is any animosity and the shopkeeper decides he does not like you, he may well decide not to deal with you – in spite of the fact that it may be to his detriment. Personal relationships are all-important.

Sport & Leisure

The Arabian countries offer an abundance of exciting sports and leisure facilities – golf, tennis, water sports, scuba diving and deep sea fishing, rock climbing, quad biking, horse and camel riding and even polo.

They are also home to several major international sporting events such as the Dubai Desert Classic golf tournament, the Dubai World Cup – the world's richest horse race – the Bahrain Grand Prix, Formula One, the Doha Tennis Tournament and many football and athletics fixtures.

Emirates Golf Club - Dubai

A popular pastime is to visit the unspoilt and beautiful desert, mountains and oases of the Arabian hinterland. However, for the uninitiated the desert can be a very dangerous place, due to breakdowns, flash floods, the extreme heat and losing one's way. It is essential to take expert advice before embarking on any trip into the desert*.

* *See* Bibliography – *The Desert Driver's Manual*.

Traditional Pursuits

The desert is equally popular with the Arabian town and city dweller. In the evenings during the cooler weather families drive into the desert for picnics and others maintain temporary dwellings and plots of land in the oases (called farms) where they camp out at weekends.

Camel and horse races are major public sporting events in Arabia.

Arabians are also passionate about horses. The famous 'Arabian' horse was first bred in the Nejd region of Saudi Arabia and by the sixth century AD breeding strains had been developed which are credited with providing the stock from which all British thoroughbreds are descended – the Godolphin Arabian, the Darley Arabian and the Byerley Turk.

One of the most ancient and highly skilled pastimes in Arabia is the art of falconry. During the hawking season – from October to April – the Arabs of the Gulf and Saudi Arabia in particular, hunt the hubaara or lesser bustard, the stone curlew and other small game.

8

Government & Business

The countries of Arabia are mostly* governed by the tried and tested traditional system of a ruler drawn from the leading family and tribe who governs by consultation and consent through a cabinet or council of ministers.

* The exception, Yemen, is now a Democratic Republic.

Members of the ruling family usually hold the key ministerial appointments of Prime Minister, Ministry of Defence, Interior, Foreign Affairs etc.

The titles of the rulers – King, Amir, Sultan, Shaikh and details of government in each country are given in the Country Annexes. In Saudi Arabia, members of the ruling family are called Prince and Princess but in the Gulf are Shaikh or for female members – Shaikha.

Over the last fifty years the rule of the Arabian governments has been benevolent and enlightened through a period of unprecedented political and economic change. They have overseen the peaceful transition of their countries from desert Shaikhdoms into independent, stable, modern states.

In the Yemen, an elected President is head of the executive and governs through a Prime Minister, other Ministers and an elected Parliament. However, the tribal influence is still very strong, particularly in areas outside the capital Sana'a.

Although further political and economic change in the region is inevitable, in the interests of stability and the wellbeing of their citizens the governments and peoples of the region wish it to take place in a planned and controlled manner, with due consideration given to Islamic norms.

Among the many future challenges facing governments in the region is that of demography. Although populations are relatively small at present – in some countries below a million – they are growing rapidly. Half are estimated to be under the age of 20 and the provision of employment for this age group in particular is a high priority.

The decision-making process in any Arab government or large Arab institution is usually tightly controlled by surprisingly few high-ranking people. One advantage of such a system is that once a major decision is taken it is often swiftly implemented. However, the Western bureaucratic system of boards and committees who investigate, consider and recommend, is being increasingly introduced as an aid to decision-making particularly in the public sector.

Foreigners in Arabia often find the functioning of Arab systems of government difficult and enlist the assistance of local agents or advisers to help with routine but time-consuming bureaucratic procedures or to access top decision-makers in business dealings. However, an agent should not replace one's own link to a decision-maker and if you decide to handle routine procedures yourself and come up against an obstacle do not lose your cool – do not attempt to browbeat anybody and never consider bribing any official. It is viewed as a very serious offence.

Business

The economies of the region are expanding rapidly in almost every field. The oil states seek to diversify from their oil, gas and petrochemical industries and major growth areas are the rising power of investment funds and financial services, property development, and an increase in free zones, tourism, sport and leisure activities.

The conduct of business may best be summarised as gentlemanly, tricky and time-consuming. The influences at work are rooted in the local culture – personal relationships are of paramount importance, social and business etiquette must be observed and religion also plays its part. Negotiating and striking a deal are conducted on well established lines and the pace is usually a good deal slower than in the Western world.

Individual success is a matter of personality and professionalism. It is important to be open, friendly and non-judgemental, able to adapt to the Arab way of doing things and to have endless patience. The Arabian businessman is generally calm and dignified, hospitable and unfailingly polite. Nevertheless he can be blunt at times and when necessary one must be prepared to stand one's ground in a firm but calm and diplomatic manner. One should also be aware that the Arabs can be great teasers and do not respect someone who rises to the bait or is easily rattled.

Professionalism means efficient market research including an understanding of the Arab culture, market and the conduct of business. There are a number of professional bodies and organisations to whom the business traveller can turn for advice and this subject is covered in detail in *The Arab World Handbook* (Peninsula Edition)*.

An Arab much prefers to deal with a foreign businessman who can act with the full authority of his parent company and does not always have to refer back to head office for confirmation of any decision.

Establishing a trusting relationship is the essential prerequisite for success in business but once established means a great deal. It takes time. For this reason the representatives of foreign firms in Arabia should be changed as little as possible.

As mentioned, the pace of life in the Arab world is a good deal slower than in the West and this is one of the most difficult things for a foreign representative and particularly his boss at home, to understand. Foreigners cannot dictate the pace of business transactions and any display of impatience will almost certainly lead to failure. Time is not money in the Arab world. Nevertheless, when a decision is finally taken, one is often expected to take swift action.

* *See* Bibliography on page 108.

Businesswomen

The business scene in Arabia may be dominated by men but there are also a number of highly successful Arab businesswomen, some controlling very large enterprises, although they often choose to adopt a low profile. Others conduct business in an exclusively female environment.

Foreign businesswomen have not found it difficult to operate in Arabia and in several fields are more successful than men. In the more conservative Arab countries however, a woman must be prepared to find men less at ease with her than they would be with a man – although she will always be treated with the utmost courtesy. For her part, the foreign businesswoman should dress soberly, not exaggerate her femininity and adopt a polite, straightforward and businesslike attitude without being in any way aggressive or assertive. In Saudi Arabia she would be escorted by a local agent or sponsor and if that is a man she should not forget that it is the custom in Arabia for men to walk ahead of women.

Western businesswomen may find it useful to consult the contacts mentioned in *The Arab World Handbook** and the advice published by UK Trade and Investment ** and other organisations mentioned in *New Moon Rising*** – a CD designed to help British businesswomen succeed in Gulf markets.

* *See* Bibliography on page 108.

** Visit www.tradeandinvest.gov.uk.

Regional Organisations

The Arab League

Formed in 1945, The Arab League exists to co-ordinate policies and activities towards the common good of all Arab states. All the Arab states of North Africa and the Middle East are members including those of the Arabian Peninsula. A large number of committees deal with a variety of sectors of interest to the League such as political, economic, cultural, social, financial and legal affairs. The Arab Monetary Fund set up by the League in 1977 provides financial assistance to member states. The permanent headquarters is based in Cairo and the League has representative offices in a number of Western countries and at the United Nations.

The Gulf Co-operation Council (GCC)

The GCC is a council of six of the Peninsula countries: the Kingdoms of Saudi Arabia and Bahrain, the States of Kuwait and Qatar, the United Arab Emirates and the Sultanate of Oman. It was formed in 1981 to strengthen relations between its members and to co-ordinate and unify policies in all fields including politics, economics and defence. It is the vehicle for establishing common systems within the GCC in such areas as finance, education, communications, travel, legal and customs and trade affairs. Its permanent headquarters is in Riyadh, Saudi Arabia.

The Organisation of Arab Petroleum Exporting Countries (OAPEC)

The Kingdoms of Saudi Arabia and Bahrain, the States of Kuwait and Qatar, the United Arab Emirates and the Republic of Iraq and other Arab oil producing countries formed this organisation in 1968 with its headquarters in Kuwait. Its aims are to safeguard the interests of its members and organise co-operation in various fields of the petroleum industry.

Notes

1. Saudi Arabia, UAE, Qatar and Kuwait are also members of the wider grouping – the Organisation of Petroleum Exporting Countries (OPEC) which co-ordinates policies on the export of petroleum to the mutual benefit of its members.

2. All the Peninsula States are also members of the Organisation of the Islamic Conference (OIC) of Islamic nations whose Secretariat is based in Jeddah, Saudi Arabia. The OIC promotes Islamic values and among other activities provides aid to Muslim communities in need.

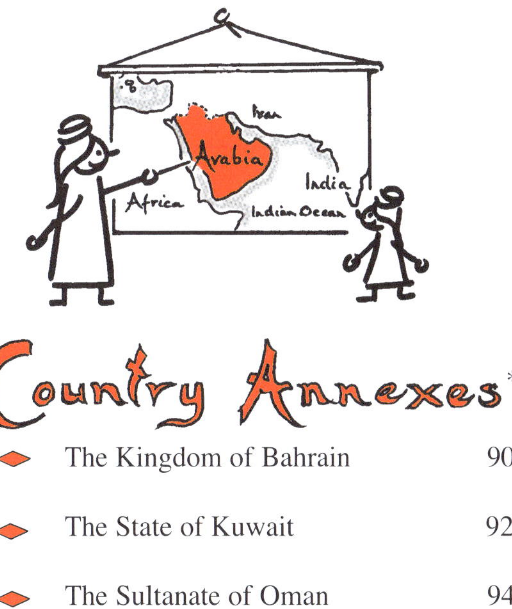

Country Annexes*

For detailed country information see the following websites:

Country Profile and Travel Advice: www.fco.gov.uk.

(UK) Trade & Investment Country Profiles: www.uktradeinvest.gov.uk.

* Please note: the maps in this section are not authoritative guides to national borders.

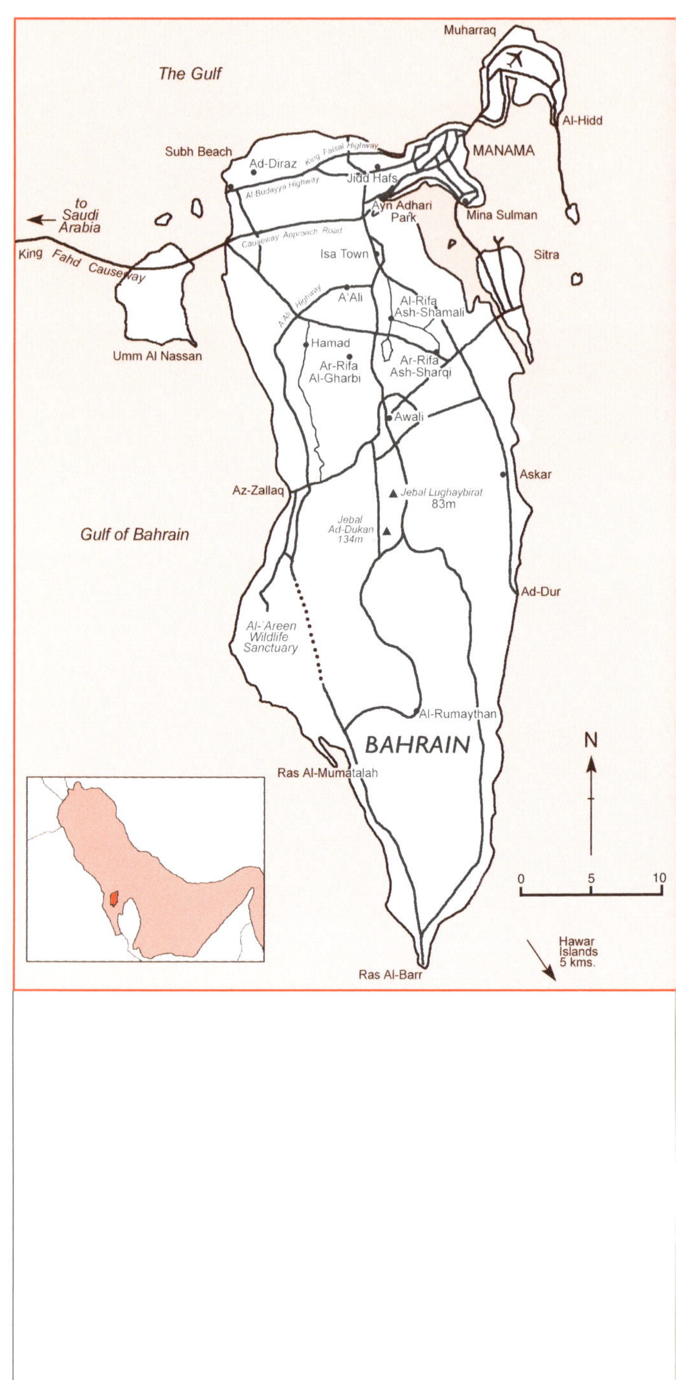
Muharraq
The Gulf
Al-Hidd
Subh Beach
Ad-Diraz
King Faisal Highway
MANAMA
Jidd Hafs
Al-Budayya Highway
to Saudi Arabia
Ayn Adhari Park
Mina Sulman
Causeway Approach Road
King Fahd Causeway
Isa Town
Sitra
A'Ali
A'Ali Highway
Al-Rifa Ash-Shamali
Hamad
Ar-Rifa Al-Gharbi
Ar-Rifa Ash-Sharqi
Umm Al Nassan
Awali
Askar
Az-Zallaq
Jebal Lughaybirat 83m
Gulf of Bahrain
Jebal Ad-Dukan 134m
Ad-Dur
Al-'Areen Wildlife Sanctuary
Al-Rumaythan
BAHRAIN
N
Ras Al-Mumatalah
0
5
10
Hawar Islands 5 kms.
Ras Al-Barr

The Kingdom of Bahrain

Geography *al-bahrain,* – 'the two seas' in Arabic, is a group of 33 low-lying islands. The largest, also called Bahrain, is linked to mainland Saudi Arabia by the remarkable 16-mile-long King Fahd Causeway. The capital city and main commercial centre is Manama which is linked to the second town and airport, Muharraq, by another causeway and bridge. The main port is Mina Salman.

Climate Pleasant in winter. Very hot and humid in summer. Minimal rain.

History Bahrain was the site of ancient Dilmun, a great civilisation and trading empire. With a strong trading heritage it was famous in more recent times for its attractive pearls, date gardens and sweet water wells. Following a lengthy period of friendly treaty relations with Britain, Bahrain declared full independence in 1971.

Government A hereditary constitutional monarchy. His Majesty the King, Shaikh Hamad bin Isa Al-Khalifa rules through a Prime Minister, an appointed 30 member Consultative Council and an elected National Assembly.

Economy With limited oil revenue Bahrain has successfully diversified its economy into oil refining, heavy industry and is a growing banking, financial services and investment centre.

Population Estimated 700,000 including 230,000 expatriates.

State Religion Islam. Majority Shi'a.

Official Language Arabic but English widely spoken.

Visas Certain nationalities may obtain an entry visa on arrival.

Alcohol Non-Muslims may import a limited quantity and it is available in some hotels and from restricted outlets for expatriates.

Local Time GMT + 3 hours, EST + 8 hours.

Dialling Code 973

Public Holidays All Muslim Festivals, New Year's Day and National Day 16 December.

Working Week Sunday to Thursday.

Currency Bahrain Dinar (BD) of 1,000 fils. Tied to US$.

US$1 = BD 0.377.

Electricity Supply 230 volts AC. Awali town 110 volts.

General A liberal but underlying conservative society: visitors should dress soberly particularly in public places. Bahrain hosts an annual Formula One Grand Prix Championship.

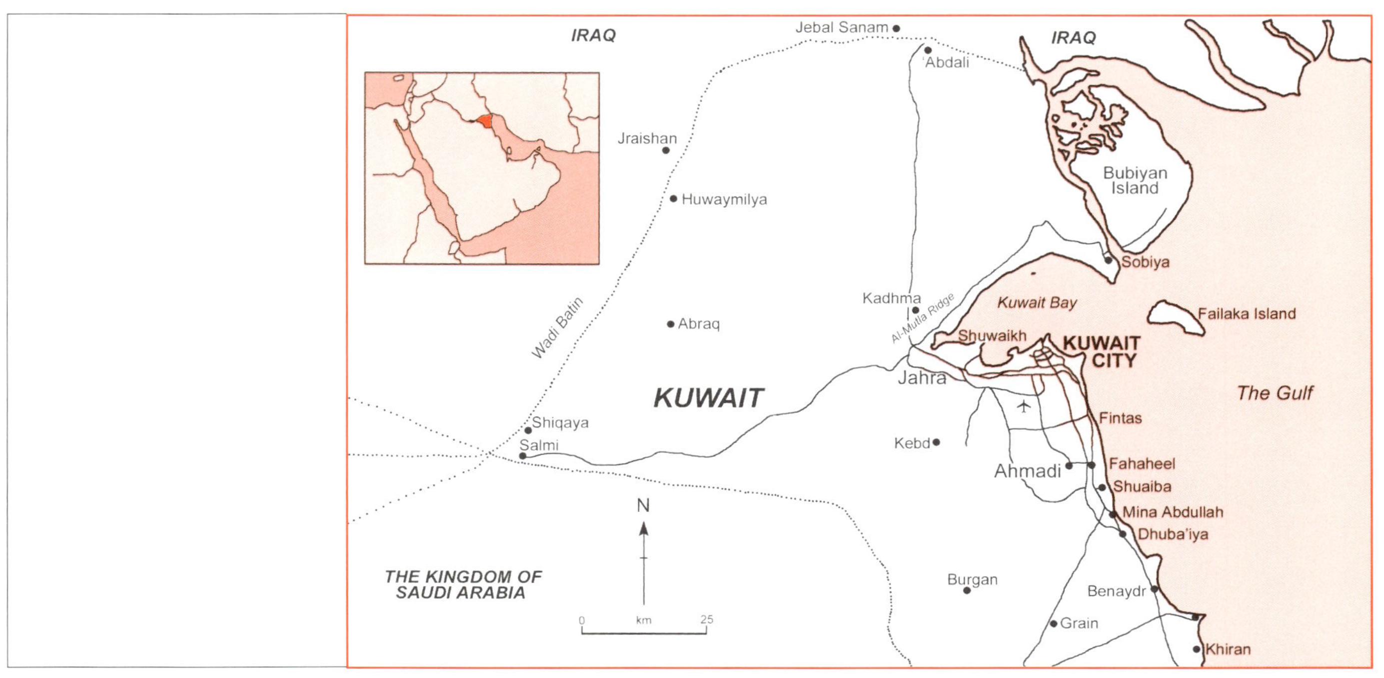
IRAQ
Jebal Sanam
IRAQ
'Abdali
Jraishan
Huwaymilya
Bubiyan Island
Sobiya
Wadi Batin
Kadhma
Al-Mutla Ridge
Kuwait Bay
Failaka Island
Abraq
Shuwaikh
KUWAIT CITY
Jahra
KUWAIT
The Gulf
Fintas
Shiqaya
Salmi
Kebd
Fahaheel
Ahmadi
Shuaiba
N
Mina Abdullah
Dhuba'iya
THE KINGDOM OF SAUDI ARABIA
Burgan
Benaydr
0
km
25
Grain
Khiran

The State of Kuwait

Geography *al-kuwait* – 'little fort' in Arabic, lies at the head of the Gulf and includes the islands of Bubiyan and Failaka. It is roughly the size of Wales. The terrain is mainly flat, arid, gravelly desert. The capital and commercial centre is Kuwait City, Ahmadi the centre of the oil industry and Shuwaikh the main port.

Climate Winter months are generally pleasant but it can be very cold at night. Summer is hot and humid. Sandstorms, particularly in early summer. Sparse rainfall usually in winter.

History Failaka island was inhabited during the bronze age and had a Greek colony in 2nd century BC. In recent history, following a lengthy period of friendly treaty relations with Britain, Kuwait declared its independence in 1961. Invaded and occupied by Iraq in 1990 Kuwait was liberated by international coalition forces in 1991.

Government Constitutional Monarchy. The Head of State, the Amir, His Highness Shaikh Sabah Al-Ahmed Al-Sabah, rules through a Prime Minister and an appointed cabinet. An elected National Assembly makes a critical examination of Government.

Economy An oil rich country, Kuwait is responsible for 3% of the world's oil production and has 9.3% of the world's oil reserves. It has substantial foreign reserves and investment income.

Population 2.3 million (est.) of whom 50% are expatriates.

State Religion Islam. Majority Sunni Muslims. Sizeable Shi'a minority.

Official Language Arabic but English widely spoken.

Visas Certain nationalities can obtain an entry visa on arrival.

Alcohol Strictly prohibited. Very heavy penalties for drugs offences including capital punishment.

Local Time GMT + 3 hours, EST + 8 hours

Dialling Code 965

Public Holidays All Muslim Festivals; New Year's Day: 1 January and National Day 25 February.

Working Week. Sunday to Thursday.

Currency Kuwait Dinar (KD or KWD) divided into 1,000 fils.

Electricity Supply 240 volts AC. Plugs flat-pin British.

General In spite of extensive mine clearing operations after liberation mines still exist in some areas, even those marked 'cleared'. It is strongly advisable to keep to paved roads outside Kuwait City.

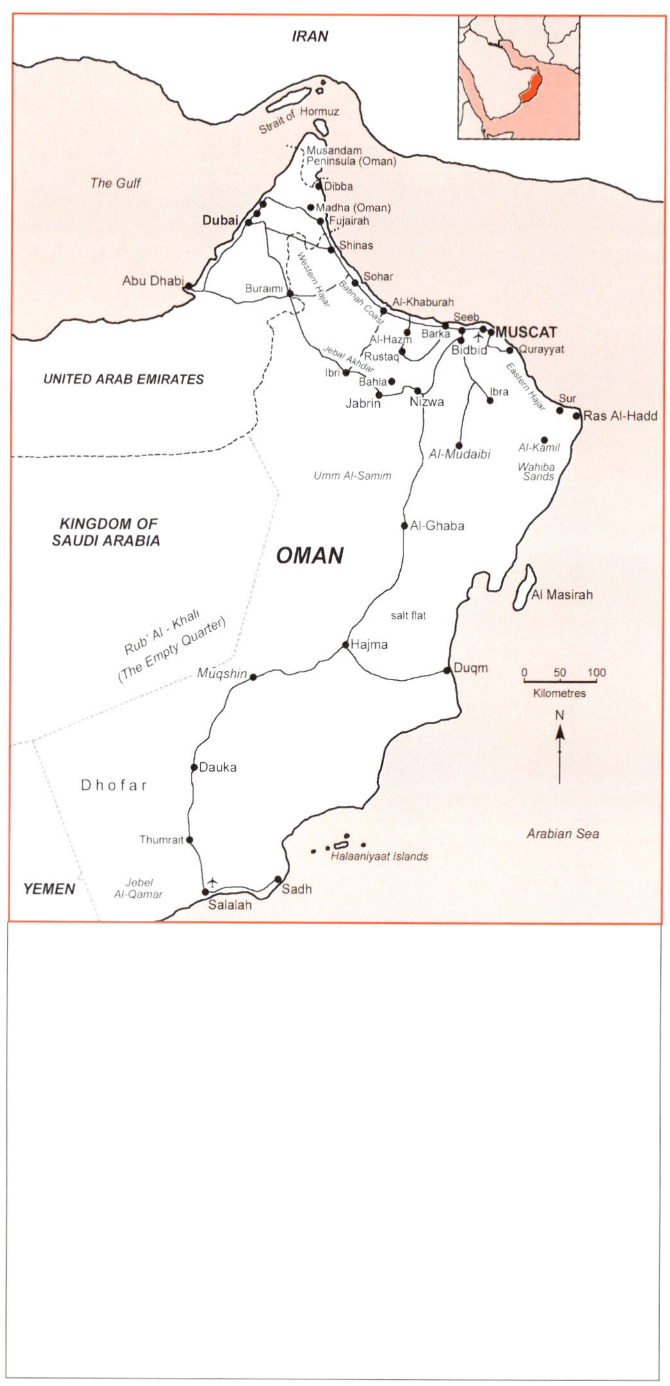

IRAN
Strait of Hormuz
Musandam Peninsula (Oman)
The Gulf
Dibba
Madha (Oman)
Dubai
Fujairah
Shinas
Sohar
Abu Dhabi
Buraimi
Western Hajar
Batinah Coast
Al-Khaburah
Seeb
MUSCAT
Barka
Al-Hazm
Bidbid
Qurayyat
Rustaq
Jebel Akhdar
UNITED ARAB EMIRATES
Ibri
Bahla
Eastern Hajar
Ibra
Sur
Jabrin
Nizwa
Ras Al-Hadd
Al-Kamil
Al-Mudaibi
Umm Al-Samim
Wahiba Sands
Al-Ghaba
KINGDOM OF SAUDI ARABIA
OMAN
Al Masirah
salt flat
Rub' Al - Khali (The Empty Quarter)
Hajma
Muqshin
Duqm
0 50 100
Kilometres
N
Dauka
Dhofar
Arabian Sea
Thumrait
Halaaniyaat Islands
Jebel Al-Qamar
YEMEN
Sadh
Salalah

The Sultanate of Oman

Geography Oman's diverse and beautiful terrain includes a 1,700-km-long coastline, the Hajar Mountains, part of the Rub' Al-Khali, the fertile Dhofar region and several islands, the largest of which is Al-Masirah. The capital, commercial centre and main port is Muscat.

Climate The interior is hot and dry except at altitude. Coastal areas are pleasant in winter but hot and humid in summer. Rainfall very low except in Salalah and Dhofar which has seasonal light monsoon rains.

History Early settlements have been traced to 3rd millennium BC. Later Oman was an important copper-producing state and a main source of frankincense. When Portuguese influence ended in 1650 Oman became independent and an imperial power in the region. Oman and Britain have long-standing friendly relations.

Government Absolute monarchy. His Majesty Sultan Qaboos bin Said rules with the assistance of a State Council of appointed ministers and an elected Consultative Council.

Economy Modest oil and gas production is the major source of revenue. Also copper and other mineral deposits. Expanding agricultural, fisheries, manufacturing and tourism industries.

Population Estimated 2.5 million, mainly Arab but also African, Baluchi, Asian, and Persian. A large expatriate community.

Religion Most Omanis are Ibadhi Muslims, but also Hindus and Christians.

Language. Arabic. English widely spoken. Also Farsi, Baluchi and Urdu.

Visas Certain nationalities can obtain an entry visa on arrival.

Alcohol Available in certain hotels and restaurants and restricted access for non-Muslim residents. Severe penalties for drugs offences including, in some cases, the death penalty.

Local Time GMT + 4 hours, EST + 9 hours.

Dialling Code 968

Public Holidays All Muslim Festivals, National Day and the Birthday of HM The Sultan – both on 18 November.

Working Week Sunday to Thursday.

Currency Omani Riyal (OMR) Tied to US$ at US$1 = OMR 0.386

Electricity Supply 220/240 volts. Plugs either 2 pin or 3 pin flat type.

General An open and liberal society but the underlying culture is conservative particularly in rural areas. Care should be taken with dress and photography.

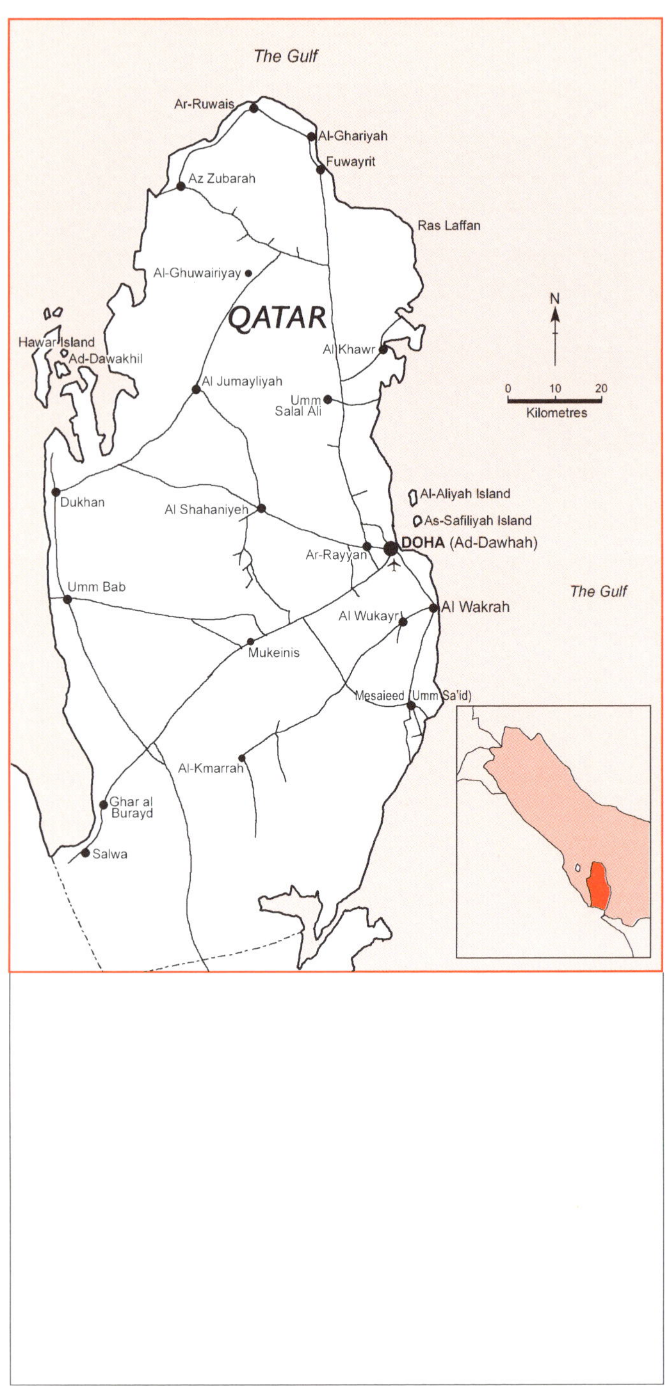
The Gulf
Ar-Ruwais
Al-Ghariyah
Fuwayrit
Az Zubarah
Ras Laffan
Al-Ghuwairiyay
QATAR
N
Hawar Island
Ad-Dawakhil
Al Khawr
Al Jumayliyah
Umm Salal Ali
0 10 20
Kilometres
Al-Aliyah Island
As-Safiliyah Island
Dukhan
Al Shahaniyeh
DOHA (Ad-Dawhah)
Ar-Rayyan
Umm Bab
The Gulf
Al Wakrah
Al Wukayr
Mukeinis
Mesaieed (Umm Sa'id)
Al-Kmarrah
Ghar al Burayd
Salwa

The State of Qatar

Geography The terrain is mainly flat gravelly desert with some low hills in the north-west and sand dunes and marshes in the south. The capital city and commercial centre is Doha (*ad-dawha*).

Climate Pleasant in winter but hot and very humid in summer. Sandstorms, especially in spring.

History Qatar (pr. 'gatter') was established in the 18th century as a traditional centre for pearling. Subsequently entering into treaty relations with the Turks and later the British, the country declared independence in 1971.

Government An absolute monarchy. The Amir, His Highness Shaikh Hamad bin Khalifa Al-Thani, rules with the assistance of an appointed Advisory Council.

Economy Predominantly based on oil although its reserves are small in comparison with its neighbours. Its natural gas resources on the other hand are among the largest in the world.

Population Estimated to be approximately 885,000 of whom 70% are expatriates.

State Religion Islam.

Official Language Arabic. English is widely used.

Local Time GMT + 3 hours, EST + 8 hours

Dialling Code 974

Visas Certain nationalities may obtain an entry visa on arrival.

Alcohol and Prohibited Substances Importation of alcohol, narcotics, pornography, pork products and religious books is strictly forbidden. Penalties for drugs offences severe. Limited access to alcohol for non-Muslims.

Public Holidays Main Muslim festivals. National Day 18 December.

Working Week Sunday to Thursday

Currency Qatar Riyal (QAR) divided into 100 Dirhams, also called Halalas. Tied to US$ at US$ 1 = QAR 3.64.

Electricity 220/240 volts AC. Light fittings – bayonet and screw. Plugs 3 pin flat most common.

General It is planned to build a causeway linking Qatar with Bahrain similar to that between Saudi Arabia and Bahrain. The Qatari Government owns Al-Jazeera, the satellite TV station which broadcasts from Qatar in Arabic and English and has a large international audience.

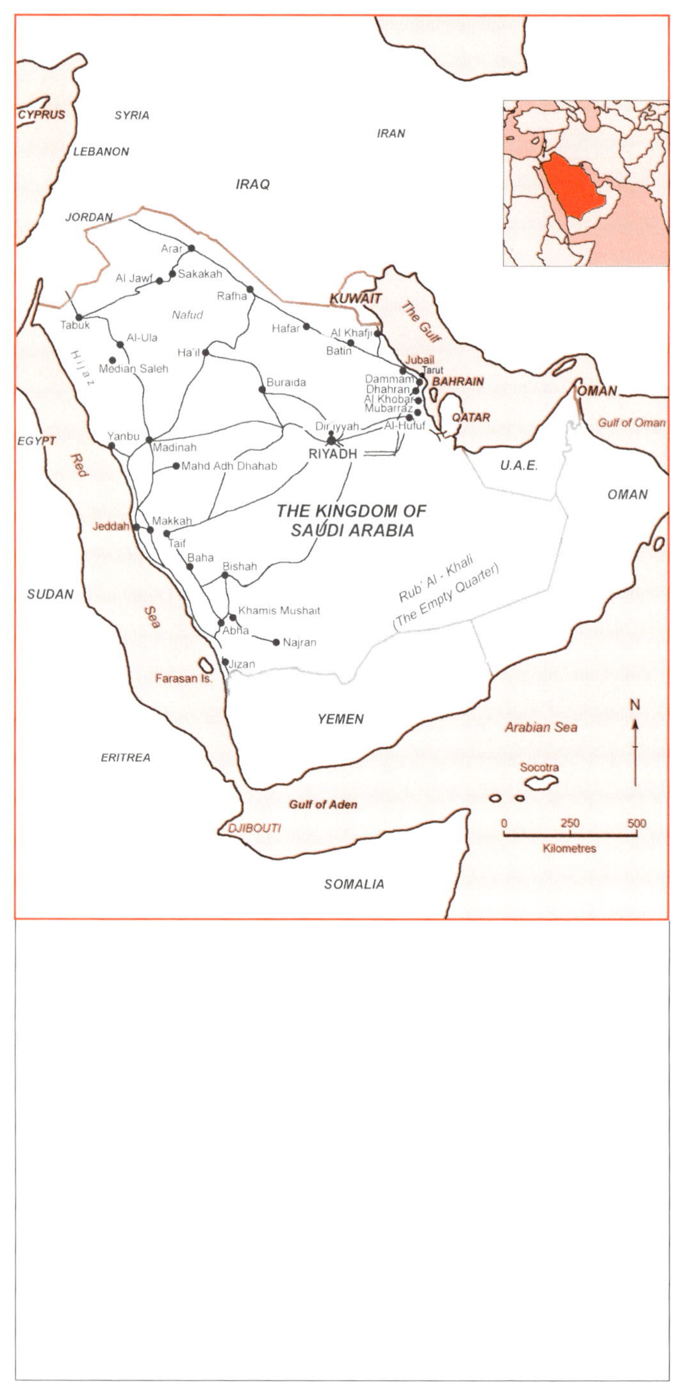
CYPRUS
SYRIA
LEBANON
IRAN
IRAQ
JORDAN
Arar
Al Jawf
Sakakah
Rafha
Nafud
KUWAIT
The Gulf
Tabuk
Al-Ula
Hafar
Al Khafji
Batin
Hijaz
Median Saleh
Ha'il
Jubail
Tarut
Buraida
Dammam
Dhahran
Al Khobar
Mubarraz
BAHRAIN
OMAN
QATAR
Gulf of Oman
Dir'iyyah
Al-Hufuf
EGYPT
Yanbu
Madinah
RIYADH
Red
Mahd Adh Dhahab
U.A.E.
OMAN
THE KINGDOM OF SAUDI ARABIA
Makkah
Jeddah
Taif
Baha
Bishah
Rub' Al - Khali (The Empty Quarter)
SUDAN
Sea
Khamis Mushait
Abha
Najran
Jizan
Farasan Is.
YEMEN
N
Arabian Sea
ERITREA
Socotra
Gulf of Aden
0
250
500
Kilometres
DJIBOUTI
SOMALIA

The Kingdom of Saudi Arabia

Geography The size of Western Europe, its varied terrain includes two huge sand deserts, the Nafud and the Rub Al-Khali, (the Empty Quarter) and two extensive mountain ranges, the Hijaz and Asir and numerous oases. The Kingdom is the location of the two holiest cities in Islam, Makkah and Madinah. The capital city is Riyadh, Jeddah is an important commercial centre and it and Dammam are the principal ports.

Climate Summer in the interior is very hot and dry but extremely cold at night. Humidity is high in coastal regions. Winter temperatures are moderate. Rain falls in winter and spring, particularly in coastal regions.

History Starting with the earliest known settlements dating from 4 and 5 millennia BC, Saudi Arabia has been home of the Nabataean civilisation, the tribal Bedu tradition, the Arabic language and is the birthplace of Islam. The Kingdom was founded in 1932 by King Abdul Aziz bin Abdul Rahman Al-Saud whose descendents still rule today.

Government Absolute monarchy. The political system is rooted in Islamic Shari'a law. The Head of State and Supreme Religious Leader is King Abdullah bin Abdul Aziz who is officially entitled 'The Custodian of the Two Holy Mosques' and not as 'His Majesty'. He rules through an appointed Council of Ministers and a Consultative Council.

Economy Saudi Arabia is the world's leading oil exporter with more than 25% of the world's proven oil reserves and the highest GNP in the Arab world. Also one of the world's largest petrochemical industries.

Population Estimated at 28 million including 7 million expatriates.

State Religion Islam.

Official Language Arabic. English is widely spoken in business.

Local Time GMT + 3 hours, EST + 8 hours

Dialling Code 966-1 Riyadh, 966-2 Jeddah and 966-3 Dhahran.

Visas By prior application to Saudi Embassies abroad.

Alcohol and narcotics, pornography and religious books other than the Quran are strictly forbidden. Drug smuggling is a capital offence.

Public Holidays *eed al-**adh**a* and *eed al-fitr* only.

Working Week Saturday to Wednesday.

Currency Saudi Riyal (SR/SAR) divided into 100 Halalah. Tied to US$ at US$ 1 = SAR 3.75.

Electricity Mixture of 110 and 220 volts with 2 pin & flat 3 pin plugs.

General The most conservative of the Peninsula states, Islamic norms strictly enforced. Shops close at prayer time. Travellers should follow closely the advice on behaviour and dress issued by their national governments.

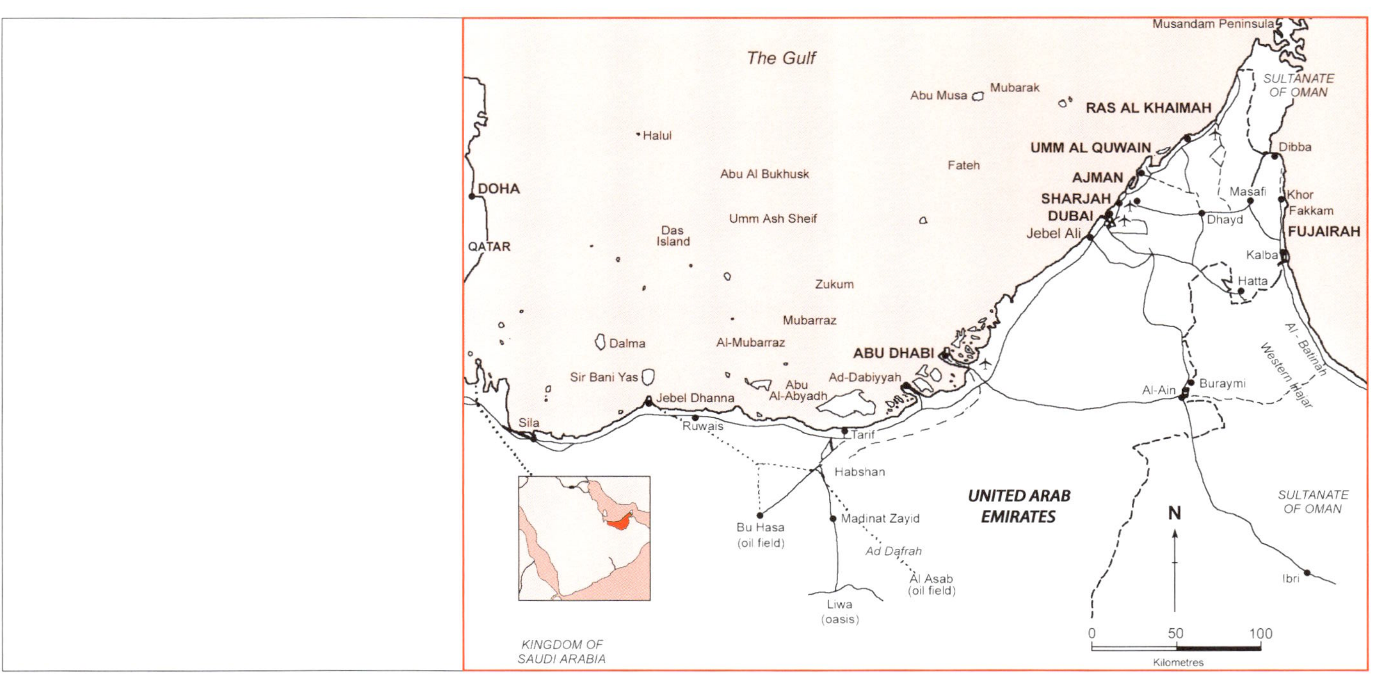

Musandam Peninsula
The Gulf
SULTANATE OF OMAN
Abu Musa
Mubarak
RAS AL KHAIMAH
Halul
UMM AL QUWAIN
Dibba
Fateh
Abu Al Bukhusk
AJMAN
DOHA
Masafi
Khor Fakkam
SHARJAH
DUBAI
Dhayd
Umm Ash Sheif
Das Island
Jebel Ali
FUJAIRAH
QATAR
Kalba
Hatta
Zukum
Mubarraz
Al - Batinah
Western Hajar
Dalma
Al-Mubarraz
ABU DHABI
Sir Bani Yas
Abu Al-Abyadh
Ad-Dabiyyah
Jebel Dhanna
Al-Ain
Buraymi
Sila
Ruwais
Tarif
Habshan
UNITED ARAB EMIRATES
SULTANATE OF OMAN
N
Bu Hasa (oil field)
Madinat Zayid
Ad Dafrah
Al Asab (oil field)
Ibri
Liwa (oasis)
0
50
100
Kilometres
KINGDOM OF SAUDI ARABIA

The United Arab Emirates

Geography A federation of seven autonomous Shaikhdoms: Abu Dhabi, Dubai, Sharjah, Fujairah, Umm Al-Quwain, Ajman and Ras Al-Khaimah. Abu Dhabi, the largest Emirate has 85% of the land area. The terrain is mainly desert with coastal salt flats (*subkha*) and two oases, at Buraimi and Liwa. The capital city is Abu Dhabi and the second largest Emirate, Dubai, is the major trading, commercial and tourist centre.

Climate Pleasant in winter. Hot in summer with high humidity. Occasional heavy rain in December and January.

Recent History Following treaties with the British in 18th and 19th centuries when the area was known as the Trucial States, the federation was formed in 1971 under the leadership of the ruler of Abu Dhabi, the late Shaikh Zayed Bin Sultan Al-Nahyan.

Government A Federal Supreme Council of the rulers of the seven Emirates who elect the President, a Council of Ministers and a 40 strong Federal National Council. The President is Shaikh Khalifa Bin Zayed Al-Nahyan, ruler of Abu Dhabi. The Vice-President and Prime Minister is Shaikh Mohammed bin Rashid Al-Maktoum, ruler of Dubai.

Economy Predominantly based on oil, gas, petrochemicals, manufacturing and construction. Abu Dhabi has 10% of the world's proven oil reserves, 5% of gas reserves. Also large investment income.

Population Estimated at 3.48 million of whom 80% are expatriates.

Religion State religion is Islam.

Official Language Arabic. English is widely spoken.

Visas Certain nationalities can obtain an entry visa on arrival.

Alcohol Available but banned in Sharjah. Penalties for drug offences severe and can carry the death penalty.

Local Time GMT + 4 hours, EST + 9 hours

Dialling Codes Abu Dhabi: 971 2; Dubai and Jebel Ali: 971 4; Sharjah and Ajman: 971 6; Ras Al-Khaimah: 971 7; Fujairah: 971 9.

Public Holidays All Muslim Festivals, Easter and Christmas, New Year's Day, Ruler's Accession Day 6 August, (Abu Dhabi only) and National Day 2 and 3 December.

Working Week Sunday to Thursday.

Currency UAE Dirham (AED) divided into 100 fils. The AED is tied to the US$ at US$1 = AED 3.672.

Electricity Supply 240 volts in Abu Dhabi and 220 volts in other Emirates. Plugs are either three-pin flat or round.

General Although a liberal society the underlying Arab culture is conservative. Visitors are expected to respect the Islamic norms in their general behaviour and dress in public.

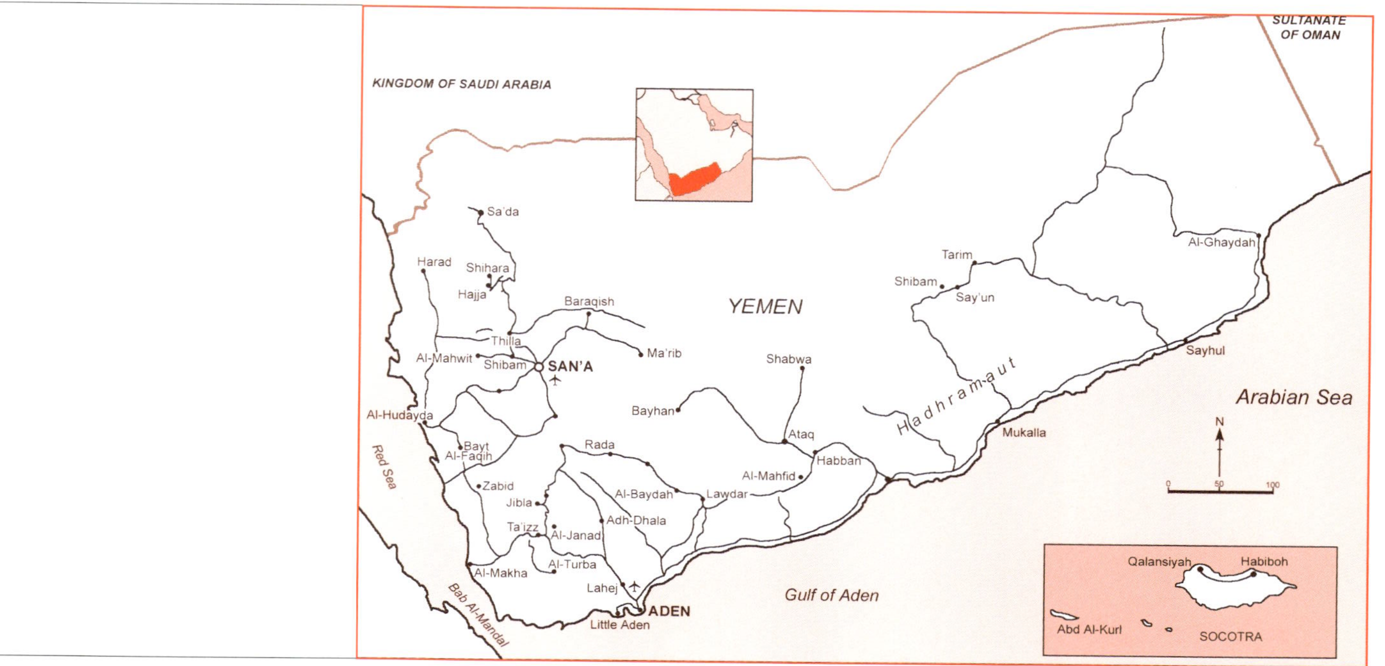

KINGDOM OF SAUDI ARABIA
SULTANATE OF OMAN
YEMEN
Sa'da
Harad
Shihara
Hajja
Baraqish
Thilla
Al-Mahwit
Shibam
SAN'A
Ma'rib
Al-Hudayda
Bayt Al-Faqih
Red Sea
Zabid
Jibla
Ta'izz
Al-Janad
Al-Makha
Al-Turba
Lahej
ADEN
Little Aden
Bab Al-Mandal
Rada
Al-Baydah
Adh-Dhala
Lawdar
Bayhan
Shabwa
Ataq
Habban
Al-Mahfid
Gulf of Aden
Tarim
Shibam
Say'un
Hadhramaut
Mukalla
Al-Ghaydah
Sayhul
Arabian Sea
N
0
50
100
Qalansiyah
Habiboh
Abd Al-Kurl
SOCOTRA

The Republic of Yemen

Geography Four distinct regions consisting of the Red Sea coastal strip, the mountains and fertile uplands around the capital, Sana'a, the desert region in the east and mountains and desert in the south. Aden is the second city and main port, Al-Hudayda, the country's main Red Sea port and Ta'izz, the most industrialised city. Hadhramaut is the location of the ancient city of Shabwa, Shibam, with its famous tower houses and the Arabian Sea port of Al-Mukalla.

Climate Coastal areas are generally hot, humid and dusty and rainfall is low. The western highlands have a mild climate with seasonal monsoon rainfall and winters can be cold.

History Home to several ancient civilisations and known to the Romans as Arabia Felix due to its prosperity and the main source of frankincense and myrrh. In recent history, after a lengthy period of Portuguese, Turkish and British influence and internal conflict, the Yemen Arab Republic (North Yemen) and the People's Democratic Republic of Yemen (South Yemen) united in 1990 to form the Republic of Yemen.

Government A democracy. Head of State is President Ali Abdullah Saleh and the ruling political party is the General People's Congress (GPC). The tribal tradition remains strong, particularly in rural areas.

Economy A major economic reconstruction and development programme is supported by the World Bank, the IMF and other donors. Limited oil production makes the major contribution to the economy together with agriculture, mining and shipping and logistics industries centred on Aden's harbour and free port.

Population Estimated at 20 million.

Religion State religion is Islam.

Official Language Arabic. English is widely spoken.

Visas By prior application to Republic of Yemen embassies abroad.

Alcohol Importation prohibited.

Local Time GMT + 3 hours, EST + 8 hours

Dialling Codes Sana'a 967 1, Aden 967 2, Hudayda 967 3, Ta'izz 967 4, Mukalla 967 5

Public Holidays All Muslim Festivals, May Day – 1 May, National Day – 22 May, September Revolution – 26 September, October Revolution – 14 October and Independence Day – 30 November.

Working Week Sunday to Thursday

Currency Yemeni Riyal (YER) divided into 100 fils. Currency floated in 1996. Advisable to carry US$ as a readily convertible currency.

Electricity Supply 220/230 volts AC, 50 Hz, with 2-pin plugs.

General Visitors should seek advice on security & health prior to travel.

__aas__if	'Sorry.' Also *muta'__assif__* and *__af__wan*
ab	'Father'
abu saleem	'Father of *__saleem__*'
'a__bai__ya	'Woman's long black cloak'
__af__wan!	'I beg your pardon.' But in reply to 'Thank you'-'You're welcome!'
__ah__lan wa __sah__lan!	'Welcome!'
__ah__lan wa __sah__lan beek	Reply to *__ah__lan wa __sah__lan* (*__bee__kum* - in reply to more than one person and *__bee__kee* to a woman)
__ai__wa	'Yes' also *na'am*
al-haajj	'The pilgrim'. Title given to a man who has been on the Pilgrimage to Makkah
al-__ham__dooli__llah__ bi-__khair__	'Praise be to God - well!' Reply to 'How are you?'
al-ja__zee__ra al-ara__bia__	'The Arabian Peninsula'
__al__lah yu__baa__rak feek	Reply to *eed mu__baa__rak*
__ash__hadu al-laa il__laa__ha illa __al__lah, wa __ash__hadu anna mu__ham__madan ra__sool__ al__lah__!	The Muslim's creed 'I testify that (there is) no god but the God and I testify that Muhammad (is the) Messenger of God!'
a__shu__ra	'Shi'a day of remembrance on the anniversary of the martyrdom of Hussain.'
as-sa__laam__ a__lay__kum	General greeting. 'Peace be upon you.'
a__yaa__mak sa__eeda!__	Alternative reply to *eed mu__baa__rak!* 'May your days be happy.'
bak__sheesh!__	'A tip!' (begging)
__bay__tee __bay__tak	'My house is your house'
bin/bint	'Son of'/'daughter of'
bi-__sur__'a!	'Faster!'
bisht	'Black, brown or fawn-coloured cloak'
__bur__qa	'Rigid mask covering woman's nose and mouth'- in the Gulf countries or – 'a gauze veil covering the whole face in Afghanistan'
__dish__dasha	'Long loose white cotton robe'

eed	'Festival'
*eed al-**ad**ha*	'Festival at the end of the Pilgrimage'.
eed al-fitr	'Festival at the end of the fast of Ramadan'.
*eed mu**baar**ak!*	Greeting at *eed* time. *Lit.* 'Blessed *eed!*'.
*fee **imaan** al**lah***	'Goodbye'. *Lit.* ' In the protection of God' (also *ma' as-sa**laam**a*)
*fee **imaan** al-ka**reem***	'In the protection of the generous one (God)'. Reply to *fee **imaan** al**lah**.*
*fee wi**daa'at** al**lah***	'In God's light.' Alternative reply to *fee **imaan allah**.*
***fut**ah*	'Brightly coloured sarong'– worn by men in Asir and Yemen
***ghut**ra*	'Men's head cloth'
*ha**deeth***	'Recorded sayings and deeds of the Prophet'
hafla	'A party'
hajj	'Pilgrimage'
***haj**ji*	Informal title of a man who has been on the Pilgrimage.
*haj**jia***	Informal title of a woman who has been on the Pilgrimage.
*hi**jaab***	'Veil'
hijra	'Migration.' The official start of the Islamic era – Anno Hijra or AH
ibn	'Son of'
imaam	'Prayer leader'
*in**sha'**allah*	'If God wills'. Common reply to statement of future intent acknowledging God's will over all things. *Lit.* If (it is) the will (of) God.
*'i**qaal***	'Black head rope'
***kaa**tib*	'A clerk'
***ka**'ba*	Cube shaped building in the Grand Mosque in Makkah holding the sacred Black Stone.
*kayf **haa**lak?*	'How are you?' (to a man)

kayf ***haa****lik?*	'How are you?' (to a woman)
kelim	'A flat weave rug'
*kha****leefa***	'Successor'
khan*jar*	'A dagger' (Oman)
*ki****taab***	'A book'
*ku****feey****a*	'Men's head cloth'
*kum****maar***	'Omani woven and decorated hat'
la	'No'
*lailat al-****mi****'raj*	'The Prophet's night journey to heaven via Jerusalem'
*ma' as-sa****laam****a*	'Goodbye.' *Lit.* 'In safety'
mak*tab*	'An office'
mak*taba*	'A library or bookshop'
*mash****koor***	'Thank you'
*masaa' al-****khair***	'Good afternoon/evening'
*masaa' an-****noor***	Reply to *masaa' al-****khair***
mas*jid*	'Mosque'
maw*lid an-nabi*	'The Prophet Muhammad's birthday'
mih*raab*	'Niche in a mosque indicting the direction of the Grand Mosque in Makkah'
min*bar*	'Pulpit' – in a mosque
*mi****naar****a*	'Minaret'
*min****fad****lak*	'Please'
*mu'****adhdh****in*	'Muezzin'
*mur****huba***	'Hello!'/'Welcome!' The *u* is pronounced as in 'but'
*murhuba****tayn***	'Two *mur****huba****s*'
*mu****salla***	'Prayer hall'- of a mosque
*muta'****assif***	'Sorry.' Also ***aa****sif* and ***af****wan*
*ma****naara****/* ***mi'****dhana*	'Minaret' - Mosque tower
*min****fad****lak*	'Please' (*min****fad****lik* to a woman)
*mu'****adhdh****in*	'Muezzin' - caller to prayer
na'am	'Yes' – also ***ai****wa*
*nar****geel****a*	'Hookah or Hubble bubble'
*ni****qaab***	'Veil covering the whole of a woman's face except for the eyes'
qib*la*	'Direction of the Grand Mosque in Makkah'
ramadhaan	'Ramadan.' The month of the Fast
ras as-sana	'The Muslim New Year'

*sab**aah** al-**khair***	'Good morning'
*sab**aah** an-**noor***	Reply to 'Good morning'
*sa**jaa**da*	'Prayer hall of a mosque'
*sal**ah***	'Prayer'
sawm	'Fasting'
sawm ramadhaan	'The fast of Ramadan'
***say**yid/**say**yida*	'Mr/Mrs'
*sha**haa**da*	The declaration of faith. *Lit.* 'bearing witness'
***shar**i'a*	'Islamic law'
***shee**sha*	'Hookah or Hubble bubble'
*she**maag***	'Men's head cloth'
shi'at ali	'The party of Ali'
***shuk**ran*	'Thank you'
sooq	'Market'
***sub**kha*	'Salt flat'
***suf**ra **da**'ima*	' May your table always be spread'
***sun**na*	'customary or orthodox procedure' or 'the practice of the Prophet'
sura	'Chapter'
*ta'**aal**!*	'Come!'
*ta**fad**dal*	'Please sit down'. *Lit.* 'Be pleased to'
***tai**yyib*	'Good'
*taa**qeeya***	'White cotton skull cap'
thobe	'Long loose white cotton robe'
umm	'Mother'
*umm sa**leem***	'Mother of *sa**leem***'
*wa **alay**kum as-sa**laam***	'and on you peace' Reply to *as-sa**laam** **alay**kum*
***wal**lah!*	'By God!'
wudu	'Ritual ablution before prayer'
*ya **ah**med!*	Polite form of address. *Lit. 'Oh* Ahmed.'
zakat	'Alms tax'

Bibliography

For further study of the history, culture and language of Arabia and the Arab World the reader's attention is invited to the following titles:

Allen, Mark (2006) *Arabs* (Bodmin, MPG Books).

Hawley, Donald (1996) *Manners and Correct Form in The Middle East* (Michael Russell [Publishing]).

Hourani, Albert (1991) *A History of The Arab Peoples* (London, Faber and Faber).

Hitti, Philip (1968) *The Arabs, A Short History* (London, Macmillan).

Nutting, Antony (1964) *The Arabs* (New York, Clarkson N. Potter).

Lonely Planet Publications (2004) *Arabian Peninsula*.

Peters, James (2005) *The Arab World Handbook – Arabian Peninsula Edition* (London, Stacey International).

Peters, James (2006) *Very Simple Arabic* (London, Stacey International).

Peters, James (2007) *Very Simple Arabic Script* (London, Stacey International).

The following titles published by Stacey International may also be of interest:

Beardwood, Mary (2004) *The Children's Encyclopaedia of Arabia*.

Chaddock, David (2006) *Qatar – Business Traveller's Handbook, (Gorilla Guides)*.

Cuddihy, Kathy (2006) *Saudi Customs and Etiquette*.

Hawley, Donald (2006) *Courtesies in the Gulf Area*.

Mead, Andrew (2006) *Saudi Arabia – Business Traveller's Handbook, (Gorilla Guides)*.

Nicholson, James (2007) *The Hejaz Railway*.

Parry, Richard, (2000) *The United Arab Emirates – Business Traveller's Handbook (Gorilla Guides)*.

Stabler, Jim (1997) *The Desert Driver's Manual*.

Notes

Notes

Notes

Notes